FAITH FOOD

DEVOTIONAL

by Wings International

Faith Food Devotional
English

© 2021 by Wings International
ISBN 978-1-7360139-0-8

Edition 1, Printing 1
5,000 copies

Biblical quotations are from the AMP, ASV, CEV,
ESV, ISV, GNT, MSG, NASB, NIV, NKJV, NLT.

Written by Becca Giles, Becky Blanchard, Ben Lawalata,
Chantel Garza, David Blanchard, Donna Blanchard, Fero Permatasari,
Ismael Garza, Kelly Lawalata, Kim Lunn, Ria Lowing, Ricardo Rayon,
Rob Giles, Rodney Richard, Stephen Walter, Steve Lunn,
Taryon Crawford, Vanessa Birkbeck.

Cover Design and Typeset by Ben Lawalata

Published by Wings International
info@wings-international.org

For more information about Wings International please visit
www.wings-international.org

Printed in Indonesia

CONTENTS

iii

CONTENTS

v

INTRODUCTION

This devotional was written by the Wings International Team (both Staff and Board members), and is meant for believers in all seasons of their walk with God. You're about to read stories of how God's Word has been alive and real in our lives — and in similar ways can be alive in yours too. We all have different backgrounds, are from all over the world, and are at different seasons in our faith journey serving God. Our prayer is that your faith and hope will be built up as you read. May you be encouraged that if Jesus did this for us and through us, he can do the same for you!

Becky and the Wings International team.

WHAT ARE YOU STANDING ON?
by Becky Blanchard

> "'Lord, if it's you,' Peter replied, 'tell me to come to
> you on the water.' 'Come,' he said. Then Peter got down
> out of the boat, walked on the water and came toward
> Jesus."
>
> Matthew 14:28-29 (NIV)

What do you have to stand on when everything else has been taken out from under you? Decisions for the future, not backing out on a step of faith you've made, losing a job, a suffering economy, sickness, family issues, etc, etc. These are all examples of times in life where our footing can be unsure.

When I was reading this Bible passage in Matthew, I was reflecting on what it means to us today. I mean, sure, if God wants us to walk on water or air for that matter, as a sign or a miracle or something to bring others to Him, go for it! But you know, when you think about it Peter really had nothing to stand on. Water isn't something anyone can stand on, but he was standing! What was he standing on?

The absolute only thing he had to stand on when he walked out onto the water was the words of Jesus, "Come." Put it plainly, he was literally only standing on the Word of God!

When heaven and earth pass away, there is only one thing that remains: God's Word (See Matthew 24:35). When everything else in our lives seems to fall apart, what do we even have to stand on? But we have this assurance that when we are walking with Him, we always have something firm to stand on. His Word will never fail us. When we go through life trials and unexpected circumstances, we can walk through them and come out on the other side still standing. We can be sure about the decisions we make today for our future when our starting standing point is what God has said in the Bible. The only way we ourselves start to cave in is when we forget this and think that what we see, and our circumstances, are what give us our footing in life, our security.

However, we need to also realize that God's Word alone is not what enabled Peter to stand on the water. It was his hope and belief in that word that Jesus spoke. Peter placing his hope in what Jesus said made

Faith Food Devotional

him able to stand on something that was physically impossible to stand on.

Friends, let's remember His Word is certain, it is sure, and it is true. Whenever you're at a place where you feel you have nothing else to stand on, put your heart's faith in what He said. And even when you're doing fine in life, make sure God's Word is what you're standing on the whole time.

2

HE MAKES A WAY
by Kim Lunn

"Be anxious for nothing, but in everything by prayer and supplication, with thanksgiving, let your requests be made to God."

Philippians 4:6 (ESV)

3

One day, my husband Steve and I were staring at each other wondering what to do. We only had 50,000 rupiah left in our bank account (approx. US$4.00). We had moved to Bali, Indonesia because God said 'go' and here we were with 3 kids to feed, our rent was due, and there was barely even enough money for a last meal. What could we do? The only thing we knew how to do.

Steve called the children in and said, "Today needs to be a miracle day." We bowed our heads and prayed. "God, we have no money left, we don't know what to do, but we trust You." How many times do we say 'I trust You' and not really mean it? Doubt creeps in and we get scared and falter, "I think I will take it back." 'Trust' is a big word, one that is easily spoken until life throws something at us that we can't handle. That's when we have to say to Jesus, "I trust You anyway."

We asked Jesus for His wisdom and began to look for jobs that would suit us. Amazingly, Steve walked into a school and they were actually hiring in the middle of the school year. Now that is trust. They were so excited to have us teaching there! They had been praying for people to come that had a desire to reach people for Jesus. His timing was perfect and the only thing we could say was that it was a miracle. They also received a miracle with us that day too. Not only did God provide us with a job, but that very day we were given enough money to pay our rent and had enough to eat for the rest of the month.

Sometimes our circumstances don't make sense until we see the whole picture. With God all things are possible. He will give you peace in the middle of the storm and guide you when there seems to be no way. What are you waiting for? Trust in Jesus. Ask Him to give you wisdom and guide you. He will never leave you and will always help you find a way.

SAME SPIRIT
by Rodney Richard

"The Spirit of God, who raised Jesus from the dead,
lives in you. And just as God raised Christ Jesus from the
dead, He will give life to your mortal bodies by this same
Spirit living within you."

Romans 8:11 (NLT)

"But you belong to God, my dear children. You have
already won a victory over those people, because the
Spirit who lives in you is greater than the spirit who
lives in the world."

1 John 4:4 (NLT)

When I transitioned into the lead pastor role, I had a crisis of identity. I was following in the footsteps of my father. He was a great leader and pastor for 42 years. Our church had multiplied under his leadership and many lives had been impacted for the Kingdom because of his leadership. I started to feel inadequate. I felt unqualified, unproven, and nervous. For the first few months, I couldn't sleep well. I felt intimidated when it came to making big decisions. The fear of trying to live up to my father felt like it was too much. People were telling me that I was doing a great job and that they loved my leadership, but inside of me, fear had crept in. During my devotion time one morning, I read Romans 8:11 and I heard the words, "Same Spirit." I heard God say, "Rodney, you have the same Spirit that I used to raise Jesus from the dead living in you. You have the same Spirit that I put in your father dwelling in you. You are the container of my Spirit." My identity crisis had been about WHAT I didn't have instead of WHO I had inside of me. This single idea started to change everything. When I read the Bible now, I can see it so clearly. When I see things like "the Fruit of the Spirit," "Power of God," and "Man of God," now I understand. The fruit is God's. The power is God's and I am God's man for this job.

You are God's person for whatever He has called you to. You have the same Spirit that raised Jesus from the dead dwelling in you!

ENCOUNTERS WITH JESUS
by Chantel Garza

> "If you have faith when you pray, you will be given whatever you ask for."
>
> Matthew 21:22-24 (CEV)

> "In the last days, God says, I will pour out my Spirit on all people. Your sons and daughters will prophesy, your young men will see visions, your old men will dream dreams."
>
> Acts 2:17 (NIV)

Have you been praying for someone close to you for their salvation, healing, or breakthrough? No matter what it is that you've been praying for, Jesus hears you. He will do what only He can do in His perfect timing. Don't give up! Continue to pray with faith and conviction that He is good!

We as a team have been constantly praying for the children and families in Bali, Indonesia that they would have dreams, visions, and encounters with Jesus. We pray for this to happen in areas that are mainly Hindu and Muslim where they really haven't had any context of what it's like to encounter the reality of Jesus. We've seen God answering these prayers of ours time and time again!

A young girl, Ayu, who we've known for 3 years from a remote village in Bali, had a dream. She went to sleep one night with a fever, but Jesus came to her in a dream. He took her hand and touched her forehead and healed her. She woke up totally healed. We asked Ayu, "How did you know that it was Jesus?" "I just knew it was Him when I saw Him. There was brightness all around, and He was bright." Since that dream, she has been watching children's Gospel videos on YouTube, reading the Bible with us, and asking many more questions about Jesus.

Ibu Ketut, who is part of our mother's skills training group, gave her life to Jesus during one of our training sessions. She went back to her village for family gatherings but had to return to the city because they had run out of food. We heard she had returned, and were so excited to go and meet her and encourage her. This was when the COVID19 season began, and we had started to bring food packages to families as most all parents had lost work. When we arrived, she expressed to us that Jesus gave her a dream. Before we even contacted her, she dreamt of us all coming to visit her. Jesus is so personal! He knew that she would be worried about food, and He gave her a dream to tell her in advance that we would come to help.

As we went out visiting another mother and her family, this mother shared with us her dream. There were two paths in front of her. The path on the right led to a crystal clear, refreshing pool of water that she really wanted to go to. The path to the left led to a dark cemetery. She took the path to the cemetery. When she arrived in the cemetery, someone came to her in need and begged for her help, but all she had to give was a dried up bone. That day, the team shared with her the story of the Samaritan woman by the well who encountered Jesus, the Living Water. She was so touched by Jesus' love for her that she put her faith in Him that day. The following week, through another dream, she was told that she must find the pool of refreshing water. And, later in her dream, she did find the water! She prayed that day to receive the Holy Spirit into her life.

Be encouraged today to surrender the people who God has placed on your heart to Jesus! He loves them even more than you do! Trust His timing, and remember that Jesus wants people to encounter Him. Let these testimonies encourage you to know that, just as Jesus revealed Himself to these people, He can do the same for all those that you've been praying for.

6

RAISE THE DEAD. WHO, ME?
by Donna Blanchard

"Heal the sick, raise the dead, cleanse those who
have leprosy, drive out demons. Freely you have
received; freely give."

Matthew 10:8 (NIV)

How many times have you read your Bible and read these words and
thought, "Wow, I want to do that!" I have many times. I remember when
I was nine years old I began talking to Jesus like a real friend. When I
was sixteen, I went to a church camp and I was introduced to the Holy
Spirit's power and began to walk with God in a different way. The Bible
came alive after I was filled with the Holy Spirit. I began to see God
do miraculous things but "raise the dead?" That was something that
seemed like only the "super pastors/ministers" could do.

I remember the first dead person I ever prayed over was with my
husband. Nothing happened. Then, another time was for my nephew,
but he did not come back to life either. I had a desire to be used by God
to raise the dead, but little by little, that topic got further and further
into the distance of my faith. Now, fast forward many years later, in
2006 I had my second opportunity to pray for someone who died. It was
my mom. I was with her when she had a massive heart attack. As I was
praying over her and rebuking death, I remembered her words just a few
months earlier, "When I die, don't bring me back." So I let her go. The
following year, in 2007 there was a third tragic accident where a large
gate fell on the wife of one of our teachers. I was called to the hospital,
and I prayed over Claudia for about 30 minutes until the doctors told me
I had to stop. Claudia stayed in Heaven.

The fourth time was with one of our Bible school students in 2009.
Lucero was on a medical mission trip with us. We had just finished our
last day of clinics and we were all washing up for dinner when someone
came to me and told me, "Lucero has fallen." I wondered why they just
didn't help her up as I walked toward her lifeless body. I quickly took
her pulse, but I could not find one. I listened for a heartbeat—none.
Just before I started CPR, I rebuked death. Each time in between chest
compressions I took authority over death. By the third attempt, Lucero

Faith Food Devotional

came to and took a breath. She sat up and then "boom" down she went, no heartbeat. I started CPR again and kept rebuking death. She came-to again. I sat her up and then "boom" down again. I started CPR for the third time. She came up and I quickly had those around us help me put her in a chair. Her arms and legs were ice-cold as she told me that she could see a dark spirit over herself. We all bound that spirit and continued to speak life over her. I was so relieved and happy she was back! When we arrived home the next day, her son asked her, "Hey mom, what happened to you on Wednesday at 10:00 pm? The devil woke me up and told me, 'Your mom is not coming home from this trip, I'm going to kill her.' So I told the devil, 'NO, you are NOT in Jesus' name!'" That was the exact time we were praying over his mom.

In 2010, on another medical clinic outreach, we were high in the mountain villages in Mexico when I was called to the medical/dentist area because of an emergency. There was a woman who had a severe reaction to the Novocain used by the dentist. I was surprised they would call me to come with all the doctors that were in that area already. I was told I needed to get over there immediately because it was serious. When I entered the room where Ernestina was laying on the floor, I knew it was very serious! I could feel the spirit of death. As I was about halfway to where she was laying, I pointed my finger at her and these words came out of my mouth: "Young lady, this is not the day you are going to die! This is not the day you are to die!" I was not planning on saying that, but the Holy Spirit took over, praise God! Just then, the doctor at her side said with excitement in her voice, "I have a faint pulse!" We all just kept praying. I had them sit Ernestina in a chair as she slowly came to. The first thing she asked was if we had gotten the rotten tooth out, then she said that she was in the most beautiful place where the colors were indescribable. I think she was in Heaven!

There is no formula. The only thing I can say is that we must be willing to pray over the sick, the dead, the lepers, the blind, the lame, and we must be the hands of Jesus and trust him for the results. If you want to see something you have never seen before, you must do something you have never done before. The results, no matter what they are, should be to give God glory!

GRACE
by Taryon Crawford

> "Don't you know that the reason God is good to you
> is because he wants you to turn to him?"
>
> Romans 2:4 (CEV)

I've heard "grace" being described as God's unmerited favor. Or more simply put, when you receive God's grace, it's like receiving a gift that you don't deserve. I want to add that His grace is absolutely poured out through the love of Christ without being based on your good (or bad) behavior or works. The Bible says that while we were still sinners, Christ loved us and died for us (Romans 5:8).

Even though I feel like I experience God's grace every day, there was a time where I fully remember experiencing His grace at a large conference in California. It happened just after a really difficult season which seemed to last forever. I had gone through a bad relationship breakup a couple years before, and it seemed that the storms of life just kept hitting me hard. Even as a believer in Christ, because of deep pain in my heart and not understanding God during that season, I made poor decisions. In my head, I believed that I should have been punished for them. But God, instead of judging and condemning, He saw me and had grace on me. The speaker at this meeting pointed at me and told me to come forward. Just before that, during a time of worship, I felt huge barrels of oil being poured upon me, and I experienced His presence like I had never experienced before. When the guest speaker called me forward, he declared over me that I was a mother of grace to this generation. After he prophesied, two other women on his team came and described everything that had happened to me in the past and also spoke into my future. Wow, I was so amazed that God, despite my shortcomings, would call me forth in front of so many people to bless me, love me, and show that He created me with His plan and purpose in mind. That extravagant grace drew me to the feet of Jesus and gave me a deeper understanding of God's love for me.

No matter what you have gone through in life, you cannot outrun God's grace. He so intimately knows you and has a purpose and plan in mind. Whatever you do in life will not make God love you any more or any less. Receive His love today and know that Father God knows you, sees you and is behind the scenes weaving a beautiful tapestry through your life.

GOD IS YOUR SOURCE!
by Vanessa Birkbeck

"Now to Him who is able to do immeasurably more
than all we ask or imagine, according to His power that
is at work within us."

Ephesians 3:20 (NIV)

When God called us into full-time ministry, we left Africa (where
we had lived all our lives) and moved to Europe. We left with just four
suitcases, 400 US dollars, and two young children. Arriving there in
mid-winter, in a country that we hardly knew, it was a huge culture
shock. But God had called us, and we obeyed and went. After being there
for just two weeks, I found out that I was pregnant. It seemed to be the
worst possible thing at a time when we were trying to establish ourselves with such little finances. It certainly was not on our agenda to
have another baby right then.

I remember that as 'missionaries' it was really tough, and we had no
money to even buy a single item for the baby. As the months passed, my
situation became more desperate. I knew God had to come through for
me because I had no one else to ask for help. We had made a few friends
through the church we attended, but I am not the kind of person that
would tell everyone all my needs and expect them to help me. God had
always answered my needs in Africa, and as God had called us into ministry, surely He would supply. I continued to pray, but I saw no answer.
By the end of eight months, all I had for the baby was a single piece of
fabric that I had bought on a sale. At least I could sew something to
wrap the baby in. In the natural, things were not looking good.

As my due date approached, I continued to seek God and ask Him to
supply all my needs just as His word said He would. I was in a foreign
nation with few friends and no support from home. God had called us,
and He had to come through for me because I knew that He was my only
hope. My answer came as I walked into our church one Sunday morning.
The pastor's wife asked if I needed anything for my baby. I said that I
just needed a few things, but could not tell her how desperate my position really was. I did not want 'man' to be my resource center. God is my
source and always has been! He can work through people and can tell

Faith Food Devotional

them what my needs are because He is my answer, He is my provider. The pastor's wife replied, "Don't worry, I know what to do." As I walked away, this huge weight lifted off of me. I just knew in the spirit that God had supernaturally come through for me! I went into the service and praised God because I knew that He had heard my prayers and that His answer was on the way.

Three days later, our pastors visited and they brought every single thing that a mother could want for her new baby. The whole church had gotten together and organized so many baby items and given so generously that we were blessed beyond measure. I remember the pastor even bringing in a big cardboard box that contained a plastic baby bath and a bucket. To my delight upon opening it, I saw that it was the exact color and design that I had seen at the store and secretly asked God for in prayer. I had also prayed for a pram/stroller that was the same kind that I had used for my son years earlier, but which I had given away when we left Africa. God also provided that, and I was so happy. The pastor and his wife even brought in a huge old-fashioned pram with big wheels! So now we had two prams, yet I had only asked God for one! (I discovered later that my mother-in-law who was staying with us had also prayed and asked God for the kind she wanted to push her grand-child around in, and this older model was the answer to her prayer). So, here we were in our tiny little house with two prams, and this baby was doubly blessed by the hand of God before she was even born! God is so awesome! I had been given so many things that I decided to send some to my sister-in-law who lived in New Zealand who was also having a baby. So, out of the abundant provision, I was able to bless her as well.

That's how God blesses. He gives generously, in abundance, over-shooting our measure and giving to overflowing. So, whatever your need is, no matter how big, just ask God and be persistent, believing that He is your source and can do abundantly more than you could ever think or dream possible. To God be the glory for great things He has done!

12

IF YOU DON'T, WHO WILL?
by David Blanchard

"For if you remain silent at this time, liberation and
rescue will arise for the Jews from another place, and
you and your father's house will perish [since you did
not help when you had the chance]. And who knows
whether you have attained royalty for such a time as this
[and for this very purpose]?"

Esther 4:14 (AMP)

13

Queen Esther was facing a difficult decision about whether or not
she should speak to the king. A decree was made from an evil official to
destroy all of the Jews. After fasting and praying, she decided that she
must speak to the king about the sinister plan. Because of her decision
to take action, the Jewish race was spared. We can change history by
speaking up and doing what is right. It can make an eternal difference
in the destiny of one person or in a multitude of people. "God has not
given us a spirit of fear, but a spirit of power, love, and a sound mind."
2 Timothy 1:7

One day I was praying with my spirit under the patio roof in my
backyard. We were getting ready to leave on a mission trip to San Lorenzo, Mexico to preach in a crusade. As I was praying, I heard in a small
voice, "You will encounter a demon." I said, "I rebuke you, Satan. That's
not true, so get away from me." Then I began to think, "The devil would
not tell me that I was going to encounter a demon. That must be the
Holy Spirit." I began to pray harder. Later, I went inside and watched a
fiction TV show. In this episode, a man was flying in a plane and looked
out the window. He saw what he thought was a man, but it really was a
demon who jumped off the wing and went into the engine. The captain
came on the speaker and said, "Everyone buckle your seatbelts because
our left engine just burned out."

The next day we left towards San Lorenzo. We crossed through a
desert region and our van engine began to cut out. I remembered how
the Lord told me that I was going to encounter a demon, and I thought
of the TV show. I wondered if a demon got into our engine! We all began
to pray as the van limped into Monclova where we were supposed to

preach in two church services. Because we were late, we only preached in one service. The next morning, I went up to the cement roof and began to pray. I heard again, "You have not yet encountered the demon." I wondered what God meant. As we began driving that day, we turned off of the main highway to head towards San Lorenzo on the dirt road through farmland. We came to a clearing in the middle of the cornfields and we saw a garbage dump. There was a woman with a bag in her hand rummaging through the garbage to find something to eat. Her name was Carmen. She was very dirty and had matted hair. We all drove by, looking out the window at her. The Spirit of God said, "There's the demon." You think that, like a good missionary, I would have slammed on the brakes to go over and pray for her, but I just kept driving on. The Spirit of God said to me, "If you don't go back there and set that woman free, who will? I told you about her two days ago, now what are you going to do?" I told the other missionaries in the van that we must turn around and go pray for that woman. Dr. David Campos, a dentist and part of the board for our churches, said, "You can't turn around because there are cornfields on both sides of the road, and besides, you're pulling a trailer." I replied, "I'm going to turn around." So I went down off of the road into the cornfield, turned around, and came back to the woman. I called her over and she came beating her chest. She said, "I'm not right, I've killed my two daughters." I said to her, "The Lord told me about you two days ago. Do you want to get set free?" She said, "Yes I do!" We cast the unclean spirits out of her and lead her in a salvation prayer to give her life to Jesus Christ. We gave her some food and clothes and went on to San Lorenzo. In the morning, there was a knock on the door. There was a beautiful woman standing there with long black hair in a purple dress who was asking for me. I asked Dr. David Campos who she was. He said to me, "It's Carmen, from the dump!" God had totally transformed her life! She was so grateful for what God had done. I was totally amazed to see a person, literally, changed by the power of the Good News of Jesus Christ.

I often pray, "Lord, may I be at the right place, at the right time, speaking the right words, to the right people, for such a time as this." We must share the Gospel of Jesus Christ while there is still time. We must speak what God is telling us to say. If you don't, who will? If you don't do something about it, who will?

CREATED TO CREATE
by Fero Permatasari

"Many are the plans in a person's heart, but it is the
Lord's purpose that prevails."
Proverbs 19:21 (NIV)

"I praise you because I am fearfully and wonderfully
made; your works are wonderful, I know that full well."
Psalm 139:14 (NIV)

I'm a certified nurse and have served as a midwife for many years
in Indonesia. I have helped with hundreds of baby deliveries, bringing
new life in the world. It's always so exciting for me to witness and be a
part of this kind of miracle each time. You know, God put a womb in a
woman for a special purpose. Inside that womb, something very special
is created and developed within.

Now say if I told you, "Here, I'm giving you 1 billion rupiah (approx.
$68,000 USD)." Do you think I trust you or not? Why would I give that
much to you? Because yes, I trust you. Now, we believe that there is only
one God who created us and that we were all created in His likeness,
right? Well, today I want to tell you that, in a figurative sense, God has
put a womb inside both man and woman!

How would you feel if you knew somebody trusted you with 1 billion
rupiah? Would you use that according to the way the giver hoped you
would? Would you use or spend the money wisely? It's the same with
the 'womb' inside you. It has purpose and God has entrusted it to you.
Take the time to nurture and develop that which God has put inside you.
Be proud of it along with all you were given that has been designed by
God. You have been giving unique dreams, abilities, and talents. Choose
to actively be a part of that purpose of having the ability to create!

Let's pray: Father in Heaven, help me to see myself the way you have
created me and see me. Please forgive me for when I have seen myself in
the wrong way and not according to your purpose. I want to know what
your purpose was when you created me. I want to honor you and create
good things with my life by using what you gave me. Thank you Lord for
your perfectness in me. In the name of Jesus we pray, amen.

Faith Food Devotional

FAVOR AND PURPOSE
by Ben Lawalata

> "For in him all things were created: things in heaven
> and on earth, visible and invisible, whether thrones or
> powers or rulers or authorities; all things have been
> created through him and for him."
>
> Colossians 1:16 (NIV)

In the process of registering our local Bali work as an official, government-recognized organization, we often have to establish relationships and gain approval with the local authorities here first. Almost every time, this happens naturally and effortlessly. We know that God's in it, and His favor is with us. In one particular case, however, it didn't necessarily feel that way. We had to deal with a leader who was not exactly open to the idea of our ministry. It certainly felt like there was a heaviness to it.

On the day we were scheduled to meet him, I was getting ready to go when a friend texted me asking how she can pray for me. She knew nothing about what was going on. I started typing my response, asking her to pray for this meeting, for favor, and ultimately a successful meeting. Right before I press send, I felt convicted. God's purpose in this meeting was not just that it would be a successful one for me. His purpose in it was not just for a man's approval, there was more to it.

God showed me that He also had a purpose for the man who I was going to meet. God was preparing me not just so that I would have a successful meeting, but more importantly, a purposeful meeting with that man as an individual. I remembered in that moment, that I always have the favor and blessing of God on me and in me as I go about my endeavors for Him. That's simply the privilege and promise of knowing and walking with Christ. So, I didn't need to pray and ask God for His favor in this situation, but rather I could praise Him for it, even in advance before seeing it. What I should pray, however, is that God would accomplish HIS purpose in my meeting with that man.

So, I prayed that God's purpose for that man's life would be fulfilled, even as I met him that day. I prayed that he would meet and encounter Christ. As I write this, the ending to this story is still in process, but I thank God that His purposes for our organization are being fulfilled.

For all of us who are in Christ, we can confidently know that we're favored because of what it says in Psalm 23:6, "Surely goodness and mercy shall follow me all the days of my life, and I shall dwell in the house of the LORD forever."

The next time you are meeting someone, don't just pray for it to be a successful meeting for you. Believe that you're already going in with His favor upon you. Thank and praise Him for this. But, pray also for the people you meet, regardless of where they are with their faith. Ask God to reveal His heart for the people you meet because He loves them and is thoughtful about them too. Pray that your meeting with them would fulfill God's purposes in both your life and theirs.

17

MY MIND TRANSFORMED
by Rob Giles

> "Do not conform to the pattern of this world, but be
> transformed by the renewing of your mind. Then you
> will be able to test and approve what God's will is—His
> good, pleasing and perfect will."
>
> Romans 12:2 (NIV)

18

There are different spiritual battles that take place in the hearts and minds of people on a regular basis. When I've faced these spiritual battles in my own life, I've found that, for me, it comes down to this solution, it's a matter of my choice. Being a follower of Jesus, I can choose to live my life in the full blessings and provisions of the Lord, or I can choose to let the enemy take that from me. Satan tries to steal what has been given to us because of our relationship with Christ, and if we're not on our guard, he will attempt to attack the areas of our lives where we may have some weakness.

When I first became a Christian, I had a very severe problem with alcohol and drugs. Living my life for the Lord showed me that I could no longer let these bad behaviors or addictions have control in my life. Still, the enemy would trick my mind into thinking it was okay to have just one more drink and that there would be no harm in that. I found out the hard way how very untrue that was. That's why the scriptures tell us that Satan is crafty and a liar. I learned that when I gave my thoughts to Jesus and listened to his direction for my life, I experienced this transformation of my mind that it talks about in Romans 12. Again, this is a choice I made, and still make because no one is forcing me to do it. Choosing to surrender every aspect of your life (and your thought-life) to Jesus is crucial to be able to withstand the attacks from Satan.

My life, thoughts, and desires were only for the things of the world before I knew Jesus. I was only concerned about doing what I wanted to do, no matter how wrong I knew it was. I had no concern about the needs of others, and my life decisions were taking me down a very dark path. That all changed when I gave my life to Jesus. The more I surrendered my will and thoughts to Him, He took me through a transforming process. It wasn't like a switch that you just turn on and off, and that renewing process is still taking place today. The more I surrender my will and thoughts to the Lord, the more I recognize how His plan for my life is being fulfilled.

This transformation is a daily process and a choice we make to refuse to conform to the world's ways. Let Jesus in today to any place in your mind that needs His transforming work to happen. Make a choice today to surrender past untrue mindsets, thoughts, or ungodly patterns in your life; let Him renew you!

MAKING HISTORY
by Ricardo Rayon

"They will be able to handle snakes with safety, and if they drink anything poisonous, it won't hurt them. They will be able to place their hands on the sick, and they will be healed."

Mark 16:18 (NLT)

"I tell you the truth, anyone who believes in me will do the same works I have done, and even greater works, because I am going to be with the Father."

John 14:27 (NLT)

When we start walking with Jesus and develop a relationship with Him, we create history. God is the same yesterday, today, and tomorrow; and if God did something once, He can do it again.

In my life, I know that one of the certainties of God is that He is the Healer. I've seen all over the world how God heals sick people. I've prayed for Muslims, Hindus, Mexican gangsters, transgenders, rich and poor people—in a church service, random moments on the street, etc. Each of these times, Jesus has healed them because He is the Healer. Healing for the sick is one of His promises. I can tell you many stories about how God healed these people, not because I am very holy, or because of my talent or anything like that. God healed them because that's His promise for us, and He wants to use us.

One day, I was outside a store in Bali where I met a Muslim man who had a swollen arm from a motorcycle accident. I asked him if I could pray for him, and told him that Isa (the name of Jesus in the Quran) is going to heal him. After praying something very simple like, "Be healed in the name of Isa," his arm became completely normal, and all the swelling went down. We were shocked that Jesus healed him immediately! I wasn't even trying to intentionally do "ministry" that day. It was just a casual moment.

However, we also need to be intentional in praying for the sick. Once on a mission trip in Mexico, my friends and I prayed for a boy named Daniel. He was paralyzed in a wheelchair. After sharing the Gospel and praying for him, Jesus healed him and he got up out of the wheelchair. His dad and uncle were screaming, "God is real, God is real!"

Today, I want to encourage you that it is always a good time to pray for someone who is sick. You don't have to be afraid or embarrassed. Go to see someone to intentionally pray for them, or just when you see an opportunity. If you already pray for the sick, keep praying for them! And if you have never prayed for someone sick, try it! If God healed someone once, He will continue to heal today and heal someone tomorrow! God is with you!

HE LIVES IN YOU
by Becca Giles

> "Little children, you belong to God and have
> overcome them, because the one who is in you is greater
> than the one who is in the world."
>
> 1 John 4:4 (ISV)

In any continent on the planet, if you're in the Red Light District at 3AM bringing friendship and compassion to the broken, or sharing Jesus' love sitting in the trash with those who've never heard of Him before, or working with people who need to know the God who sees and cares for them individually—you carry His Spirit everywhere.

We had just moved to Bali, Indonesia, and quickly realized why it was known as the "Island of the gods". Offerings are given daily (ritually) as a thank you to their gods, and also as a request to the evil spirits to go away. Religious ceremonies are constantly happening throughout the island as it's required for the cleansing of their karma.

The house that us girls moved into was all fine, except for the almost 2.5 meters (8 ft) tall Hindu altar that was built in the back. We moved in anyway and began our lives in Bali. After living just a few days in our new home, we heard a deafeningly loud crash occur outside. We rushed to look out our back windows to see what had happened. There was an enormous heap of our tile roofing that had plummeted to the ground. It wasn't a very nice feeling to think that we had just moved into a crumbling house. We looked over to the side, however, and the once lofty, stone altar that stood tall was now completely broken in half.

We didn't have to, or want to, try to break this altar down with our own effort; we plainly lived in that house for a few days and prayed and anointed it with oil when we first moved in, dedicating the home to God. Our awareness of the Holy Spirit's presence inside of each of us that day heightened. Because of His presence in us alone, the altar (and any spirit that lives in the world) had to bow. He is unfathomably greater.

Walk into your job, or into your family who hasn't come to know Jesus yet, or into the calling on your life, being assured of this: God has given you victory over the spirit that lives in the world. And, He lives in you.

HE KNOWS WHAT HE'S DOING
by Stephen Walter

"Trust in the Lord with all your heart, and do not
lean on your own understanding. In all your ways
acknowledge him, and he will make straight your paths."
Proverbs 3:5-6 (ESV)

Most people might never get the chance to travel enough to fill up a passport, but by the grace of God, I found myself in that very situation. I had been serving with the Wings International ministry team in Bali for about 2 years, and we are fortunate enough to travel all around Asia. We normally go back to our home countries around November/December to fundraise for the next year, but this time, I was in a predicament. My visa was set to expire in September, and I didn't have enough pages in my passport to come back into the country to renew it. It was decided that I would go back to America when my visa expired, and return earlier than anyone else the next year.

On the other side of this situation, my father had been having some health complications and had gone in for minor surgery near the beginning of September. I wasn't too worried about it as I trusted what my parents were telling me, and that God had this situation under control. As I arrived back in the states, my mom told me that the surgery had gone a little awry and dad was at home resting. I had barely got my luggage through the door when I quickly went to see my dad. He noticed me enter the room, and his smile stretched from ear to ear. I gave him a hug and left to let him rest. My mom explained to me that he was supposed to be feeling better a few days after the initial surgery, but his pain level never really went down. The doctor told them that sometimes different people need longer to heal and that my dad should call every day to check-in. This had been going on for a week with no changes, and my mom was worried she would have to quit her new job as a flight attendant to take care of him. Although she kept her composure in telling me all this, I could see her holding back tears. I knew right then and there that God had brought me back at this specific time to take care of my dad. I reassured her that I could take care of him while she continued to work.

Faith Food Devotional

As my dad's first surgery hadn't taken properly, and a cyst began to form, he had to go back to the hospital for emergency surgery. I visited him in the hospital every day and stayed by his side through the pain, and the sleepless nights. God had even made it possible for my brother, who was passing through on his way to work in Canada, to stay for two months. My dad was finally released from the hospital after a month. He felt so much better, not only because his insides were back in order, but because God had brought us all together at just the right moment. I came back to America because of a visa complication, and my brother stayed in America because of his visa complications. God truly works in mysterious ways.

Sometimes we don't see the big picture of what God is doing, and we become fixated on unimportant details. God sees our lives in entirety, beginning to end, and He has mapped out His best plan for your life. Although you may not see or understand why some things may be happening, or why you are facing certain trials, God is always there to bring you through it. Have faith that God sees you, hears your every cry, and has a plan and purpose for your life.

NOT FORGOTTEN
by Becky Blanchard

"See what great love the Father has lavished on us,
that we should be called children of God! And that is
what we are! The reason the world does not know us is
that it did not know him."

1 John 3:1 (NIV)

25

"'My son,' the father said, 'you are always with me,
and everything I have is yours.'"

Luke 15:31 (NIV)

One time with my family we were in Estes Park, Colorado, just spending some quality time together in the mountains. Downtown Estes Park has a lot of cute and fun shops to visit, and some of our favorites are the shops with saltwater taffy, which is a form of candy. Because Estes is such a destination location, there's a lot of competition; so each shop gives out plenty of free samples to promote their candy. This is my niece and nephews' favorite part...and let's be real, mine too! That day, when we were walking around enjoying our samples, we decided we wanted to buy ice cream. So we walked into an ice cream shop and began requesting samples from the display counter before we chose the flavor we wanted. There were tons of good flavors to choose from! We all started taking turns requesting samples. While this was happening, my youngest nephew Hudson, who was only 3 years old, was too short and small to see over the counter to choose a flavor. He could only see us enjoying our samples. Then, all of a sudden, we heard this tiny little voice speak up, "Meeeeeeeeeeeee, meeeeeeeeee." We looked down at Hudson and realized that even though we had just arrived, he thought we forgot about him. He was watching some of us enjoy ice cream while he wasn't. Even though only a few moments had passed by, at his age, it probably seemed like an eternity, and of course, we weren't going to forget him or leave him out from enjoying some ice-cream goodness.

That memory of him makes me smile. It was so cute. He wasn't at the age where he could say many words, so the only way he could think to express, "Hey, don't forget about me," was by saying, "Meeeeeeeee."

Faith Food Devotional

And sometimes, I feel like that can be us when we see others around us enjoying the blessings and promises of God. Sometimes it can feel like we're surrounded by these scenes and start to feel like we're forgotten, like so many around us are enjoying the fulfillment of the promises of God while we're still waiting and believing for them to come to pass in our own life. Those "Hey God, what about me?" moments.

But the truth is, we are never forgotten; we're part of His family. It's always a part of God's plan for us to enjoy all of His goodness—and in His good timing. Things always look different from His angle.

Today may you be encouraged and assured of all the goodness God has in store for you!

Trust His goodness.

Trust His timing.

Trust His wisdom.

Trust His unfailing love for you.

"Alway trust, always hope, always persevere!" - 1 Corinthians 13:7

(Also, see Jeremiah 29:11 for an "Ohhh, yeaah" reminder, because we often forget or lose sight of this.)

GRADUATION FINANCIAL MIRACLE
by Ria Lowing

"Do not be anxious about anything, but in every
situation, by prayer and petition, with thanksgiving,
present your requests to God."
                                        Philippians 4:6 (NIV)

Two weeks before I graduated, I had to pay a pretty expensive graduation fee. Because I was working, I was able to fund my own tuition
while I was in college. But two weeks before graduation, I had no money
to pay for the graduation fee. I tried asking for help from the people
closest to me, but they couldn't help me at that time. I even planned
to borrow money at the bank, but I knew I did not want to have debt
entering into the new year.

I prayed and cried to God in my room asking Him for a miracle to
help me pay my graduation fee. That night when I prayed, I vowed to
God saying, "God, if you give me this financial miracle, and I don't need
to borrow money in the bank, I will give my life as a tool to be your witness in sharing the Gospel to neglected regions or tribes." The next day
after I finished work, I planned to go to my house to process the loan at
the bank. But at that hour I got a call. My friend called me and asked to
meet me right then and there. I waited for her in my office. When she
arrived, she explained to me that, as she was praying for me, God spoke
to her through the Scriptures to give me assistance for free. I was so surprised—I never told her that I needed help. When I opened the envelope
that she gave me, I received the exact amount of money that I needed
for graduation. I immediately thanked God, and surrendered my future
completely to Him.

Jeremiah 29:11 says, "'For I know the plans I have for you,' declares
the LORD, 'plans to prosper you and not to harm you, plans to give you
hope and future.'"

Before, I was very selfish—I planned my own future and asked God
to approve my plan. When I experienced the great miracle that God did,
and realized that He had a beautiful plan for my future, all of the plans
that I had composed previously became meaningless. I discarded all of
my plans, and allowed God to rewrite the pages of my life. I surrendered

everything to His plan.

One thing I can tell you is that God has a big and beautiful plan for my future and for your future too. I pray that you can surrender your life plans, and let God write the story of your future. Believe that He never disappoints. His plans are bigger than our plans, and His love is so great for us. When you surrender your life to God, you will be amazed by what happens in your life. "That is what the Scriptures mean when they say, 'No eye has seen, no ear has heard, and no mind has imagined what God has prepared for those who love Him.'" 1 Corinthians 2:9

28

JESUS, I NEED TO BE RESCUED!
by Rob Giles

> "Salvation is found in no one else, for there is no
> other name under heaven given to mankind by which we
> must be saved."
>
> Acts 4:12 (ESV)

Have you ever felt like you were in a situation or problem where you just weren't sure how you would ever get out of it? I have been there. For example, I would try whatever I thought would help fix the problem and give me a sense of peace again. Sadly, the things I tried never really helped, or maybe they did but only for a short time. This is when I learned that the only real way I could be rescued and saved was by asking Jesus into my life. When I did this, I found great joy and freedom whenever I found myself in those difficult situations or problems again. Trusting in Jesus helped me to know that I didn't have to face life's challenges on my own and that I didn't have to rely on my own ability to fix problems that would happen.

What about you? Is there something you're facing in life that seems too difficult to handle? Would you consider asking Jesus into your life? His word says that He will never leave you or forsake you. Knowing that for my life has been very helpful because now I know that I am not alone and that I don't have to rely on my own ability or power when things go wrong.

MINISTRY, LIFE, AND FARMING
by Chantel Garza

"Let us not become weary in doing good, for at the
proper time we will reap a harvest if we do not give up."
Galatians 6:9 (NIV)

30

Ministry and life can be compared to farming. Have you ever experienced a season where you have poured into people's lives, or you have personally had struggles, or you have found yourself waiting? In each season, there is a purpose for us being in it.

During the season of Coronavirus in the world, we as a team remained in Bali. We experienced many miracles of healing and provision for the families that we went to minister to. While I was just thinking of how amazing it had been being able to experience people coming to know Jesus, getting healed and baptized and praying for jobs and then having Jesus answer that prayer. I was so thankful to Jesus! We saw the power of the Gospel being made real in the lives that we were ministering too.

It was at that time that I felt Jesus share with me on how being a missionary is like being a farmer. We spent the first three years of sowing seed into an area that had never heard of Jesus, they are Hindu. Sowing the seed takes time, faithfulness, perseverance and at times it can be uncomfortable, but that season is so essential in order to experience the fruit. Once a farmer sows the seed, he watches over it and waters it and that's what Jesus has called us to do. Sow His truth, don't give up, look after the seed that's been sown in the lives of His people and He will make it to grow. That's our call as a farmer. We cannot determine the length of seasons, we just stand in hope. Hope is not a feeling, it's our focus. Our focus is on the seed that has been sown. We hope for what we don't have, if we hope for what we already have it is not hope. Now in our fourth year and in a season no one was prepared for (COVID), we were seeing growth and fruit. Being in that season is an exciting season BUT the sowing, watching, watering doesn't stop until He calls us elsewhere or says so. We continue being faithful to His call, heart of love, and promptings. This increased my faith and hope for the other areas Jesus has called us to as a team.

So I want to encourage you today to remember what Jesus has asked you to do, don't give up. Remember as you have sown that seed (in your own life and others) you know it has been planted and so fruit shall come from it in due season.

Prayer: Jesus we praise you for what you have already done and for what you will continue to do in my life and the lives of those I am praying for! Thank you Jesus for helping me see the seasons I am in through your eyes. Thank you for counting me trustworthy and appointing me to be your hands, feet, hands, and mouthpiece to those that don't know you or for those that need to be reminded of your love for them. Please give me wisdom in this season, to know what to do or say! Amen

NOT STUCK IN REGRET

by Stephen Walter

> "To all who mourn in Israel, he will give a crown of beauty for ashes, a joyous blessing instead of mourning, festive praise instead of despair. In their righteousness, they will be like great oaks that the Lord has planted for His own glory."
>
> Isaiah 61:3 (NLT)

> "He has made everything beautiful in its time. He has also set eternity in the human heart, yet no one can fathom what God has done from beginning to end."
>
> Ecclesiastes 3:11 (NIV)

Although I grew up in a Christian environment, I made many mistakes. From my struggles with alcohol abuse and drug addiction to sexual immorality, I was far from being the "perfect Christian." Many times throughout my upbringing, I felt split between two worlds. I was diligently serving in the church, and simultaneously struggling through carnality with my friends.

I remember driving with my mom about a year ago, and she asked me about my past experiences with drugs and alcohol. She asked me why I felt compelled to engage in that lifestyle and what benefits I perceived to have gotten out of it. As I explained, I could see her sense of subtle disappointment, and yet she was understanding as well. She finally asked, "Do you regret any of it?" I thought for a few minutes as I began to weigh all my past choices. I felt a peace come over me in that moment as I answered her: It's not that I don't regret those things I had done, but I choose not to live, stuck in regret, because of them. It felt weird saying this as all my past mistakes came flooding to the forefront of my mind. All the people I'd hurt, all the times I consumed poisons in the name of "fun"—but this was the truth. If I lived in regret, I don't think I would be in the place I am at the present time, serving as a missionary in Bali, Indonesia. God took what the enemy meant for evil against me, and turned it to bring me into His presence.

Many times, people say that they wish they could travel back in time to change the mistakes they've made, or "slap some sense" into their younger selves. However, it's impossible to do that. It is so much better to look at your present situation and see that God has, and is, actively piecing together the parts of your life that you thought were broken. To live in regret of what you've done is to live in the lie that your brokenness can never be made new and whole again in Christ. Jesus died so that we can be made a new creation through him. Know that your life is precious, and seize every second that God has given you to be the best version of yourself now. I praise God that He stayed at the doorway of my heart until I fully let Him in. I am where I am because, by God's grace, this is where He led me. This is where He needs me.

33

I urge everyone who reads this to thank God for all the times in your life, the good and the bad, because God can make all things beautiful. He even brings beauty from ashes. If you are going through a tough time now, believe that God has a plan for your life. Even with all the things you see as failures in your life, God can turn them all into victories as part of your testimony in Him.

FATHER FIGURE
by Fero Permatasari

"Not only so, but we also glory in our sufferings,
because we know that suffering produces perseverance;
perseverance, character and character, hope. And hope
does not put us to shame, because God's love has been
poured out into our hearts through the Holy Spirit, who
has been given to us."

Romans 5:3-5 (NIV)

"I will be a Father to you, and you will be my sons
and daughters, says the Lord Almighty."

2 Corinthians 6:18 (NIV)

When I was a teenager, I went through many situations where it seemed as if no one cared for me. In that time, I had to learn to take care of myself and I had to learn to carry on by myself. I asked for help, longing for security and even shelter, but there was none—not even in my family. I didn't really have a good male-figure to look to in my life, and this impacted the way I saw men and other people. It was hard for me to trust anyone, and I didn't see men from God's perspective. I kept everything that happened to myself, and I tried to fight every situation in my life with my own strength.

One day, I was reading the Bible and turned to Romans 5:3-5. Whether you realize it or not, God has given the Holy Spirit to us. He is there with us, always. He loves us. I didn't know at first that God was there for me until I started to see it in my own life. It has been fifteen years since that difficult season. Now, I see how God is more than enough and He has always been there for me and never leaves us alone. He has changed me, and now I can see men the way God has created them—with their design and purpose. God is the best role model of every single figure that you and I need in this life. I encourage you to look to Him and keep having hope and faith as little children.

Let's pray: Happy Father in Heaven, help me to know that you will always be there, your spirit will always be with me. I am not alone. Help me to open my eyes, ears, and heart to feel your presence that is actually right here with me. Help me to have faith like a little child and to learn to trust you more and more. Thank you for giving me this life I have and for everything good that you have given me. I love you, Lord. Amen.

DO NOT WORRY
by Ria Lowing

"Therefore do not worry about tomorrow, for tomorrow will worry about itself. Each day has enough trouble of its own."

Matthew 6:34 (NIV)

"Therefore I tell you, do not worry about your life, what you will eat or drink; or about your body, what you will wear. Is not life more than food? And the body more than clothes? Look at the birds of the air; they do not sow or reap or store away in barns, and yet your heavenly Father feeds them. Are you not much more valuable than they? Can any one of you by worrying add a single hour to your life? And why do you worry about clothes? See how the lilies of the field grow. They do not labor or spin. Yet I tell you that not even Solomon in all his splendor was dressed like one of these."

Matthew 6:15-29 (NIV)

I went through a difficult time in my life when I had just resigned and didn't have a job. Usually, I'd help my family's economy, but at that time we had no money. We had only a little rice left from our stock, and very soon it was going to run out. When I'd think of when that would happen, I began to feel anxious and sad. What will we eat when it's gone? I prayed to God who has everything to help me and my family. I didn't expect God to answer my prayer so quickly, but after one hour, I received a transfer of money into my bank account. Thank God! I felt so happy and grateful that I could buy rice for the next day's meal. I've experienced many days in my life—not just this story—where everything seems to be lacking in the eyes of man, but God always takes care of me more than the lilies in the fields.

Through these verses in Matthew, I was taught not to worry about tomorrow. Let's learn to be content, and always grateful for what we have today. Maybe you're in the middle of a difficult time, and have even experienced the same thing as me. Matthew 7:7-8 says, "Ask and it will be given to you; seek and you will find; knock and the door will be opened to you. For everyone who asks receives; the one who seeks finds; and to the one who knocks, the door will be opened."

When you face hard times, ask God for help. He is a good Father who always hears us. I pray for whatever your situation is, that the same God who helped me and my family will meet your needs according to His Word. He's our faithful father who always takes care of us. During your daily quiet time, continue to rely on God, and let your faith and hope be strengthened in Jesus. 37

A HEART'S CONDITION: AT REST VS. IN TOIL
by Kelly Lawalata

> "Don't exhaust yourself acquiring wealth; be smart
> enough to stop. When you fix your gaze on it, it's gone,
> for it sprouts wings for itself and flies to the sky like an
> eagle."
> Proverbs 23:4-5 (MSG)

I am the type of person who enjoys projects. I love many different kinds of projects and hobbies, and I really enjoy trying new things. Often, I'll have 3 or 4 completely different projects going at the same time. At the moment, I've been experimenting with gardening. In doing so, I've had to learn about growing conditions, watering levels, and the basic nutrients a plant needs in order to thrive. The more I learned, the more curious I got. So, naturally, that led me to different WAYS of gardening: soilless gardening, aquaponics, vertical growers, etc. There are just so many things I'd like to try! In my excited franticness, I started trying this and trying that. I would get supplies for aquaponics, while still not having finished planting my traditional garden. I'd get seeds for a plant that I had no plan or space for, and meanwhile, learn about how to grow something I don't even have. One day while in my garden, I found myself entirely scattered. One second I'd be working in the soil, and the next second I'd be making a compost. I was working so much on this but getting nowhere. I had too many things going at once, that I wasn't able to finish just one thing...not even the main thing. That's when God stopped me in my tracks. This simple word emerged and flooded my heart: TOIL. I was toiling.

From the Dictionary: Toil /toil/ Verb To work extremely hard or incessantly.

What God was talking to me about, wasn't that I shouldn't work hard to grow tomatoes. No, He was in fact not speaking to me about my gardening project at all. He was just using that moment as a picture. You see, in other areas of my life and in my heart I was working and striving and going and trying new things for success and selfish ambition. I carried a 'level-up' mentality. Always forward, always more. All of the ambition inside of me for life and achievements and work and success was making its way out, and I found myself toiling and toiling to achieve something. I was not resting in my heart or in my soul. Not resting in Christ. Not resting in the fact that HE is enough, and that HE is the most important and valuable thing I could ever have.

And again I was reminded of my true purpose on this earth. Yes, the very most important and fulfilling thing I could do: Know Jesus and go share Him with the world. All the rest of the things I have a desire for may or may not be added to me, but of this I am sure: Toiling makes one sick and tired. It may bring you what you're looking for in a temporary moment or season, but as the Proverb says, "it sprouts wings for itself and flies to the sky like an eagle." Success can come and go, but the thing that remains steady in every season is the profound surpassing fullness of knowing and living with Christ. He provides all my needs. He sees all my needs. I trust Him. I honor Him. I live my life for Him in every decision I make.

"Then Jesus came to them and said, "All authority in heaven and on earth has been given to me. Therefore go and make disciples of all nations, baptizing them in the name of the Father and of the Son and of the Holy Spirit, and teaching them to obey everything I have commanded you. And surely I am with you always, to the very end of the age." Matthew 28:18-20 (NIV)

Lord, let this be the ambition of our hearts and the propelling force for our efforts and work. May we not get caught up in the toiling of our hands for selfish ambition, but may we work for the cause of your glory, and find rest and contentment in your presence. Amen.

STOPPING FOR THE ONE
by Chantel Garza

"The Spirit of the Lord is on me, because he has
anointed me to proclaim good news to the poor. He
has sent me to proclaim freedom for the prisoners and
recovery of sight for the blind, to set the oppressed free."
Luke 4:18 (NIV)

We had just finished up our ministry time on the beach as we do every Wednesday night. I was just observing the parents and the children and I felt to stop and to sit with one of the mothers that attended that night. I started asking how she was and how her week was. During our conversation, the mother expressed that her right arm was in such pain that she couldn't raise it or sleep at night. I took that opportunity to pray for her arm...and guess what? Jesus instantly healed her. Her face was priceless with joy and shock. She raised her arm up and down—the pain was gone. The following night she came again to our outreach and started asking, "Why is it that when I pray nothing happens, but when you pray there is power?"

This opened a door for us to speak about Jesus' love and His heart for her. She told us also that she had slept so well for the first time in a long time—so much so that she overslept that morning! Jesus knew she needed His healing touch. He was just waiting for someone to STOP and sit with her. Let us keep this in mind: we must stop to listen or observe, and simply wait on Jesus.

Pray: Jesus, please give me eyes to see as you see, and a willingness to stop during the busyness. Let me become aware of those you want to touch, set free and love today. I desire to be your hands, feet, mouthpiece, and heart to others that need you. Amen.

HE MADE A WAY
by Stephen Walter

"Fear not, for I am with you; be not dismayed, for I
am your God; I will strengthen you, I will help you, I will
uphold you with my righteous right hand."
Isaiah 41:10 (ESV)

Music had always been something I'd been good at from an early
age. From taking piano lessons in grade school to learning the violin
and bass in middle school, there was something about it that made
sense to me. As I continued with the orchestra through high school, I
had amazing opportunities to play music with incredibly talented individuals. I loved the feeling I'd get when a group of people created one,
beautiful, sound. This feeling, coupled with my director's passion for
teaching music, gave me the inspiration to pursue a degree in music
education. I was fortunate enough to have quite a renowned music program at the university in my hometown. Although it may have seemed
odd to some, this university was the only one I applied to. By the grace
of God, I was accepted; but this didn't mean I was accepted into the music program. I then began having weekly, private lessons with the bass
professor to prepare for the audition to get into the music program. I
had never done an audition before, and the quality of the piece he had
chosen for me was more difficult than any other I had played before. I
practiced every day, but I felt like there was a mountain of skill that I
couldn't get over—no matter how hard I seemed to try. I began to stress
about my audition. I was scared that I would not only be letting myself
down, but my parents as well because of how much they believed in me
and invested in my future. Stress made its way into my practice time,
and I couldn't focus without being overwhelmed with anxiety every
time I made a mistake.

The day of my audition finally arrived. I was trying to stay as calm
as possible (which was easier said than done). I began to feel sick with
such anxiety that I went to my room and began to pray. I pleaded with
God to take away this feeling so I could audition with a clear head. I
remember repeating, "Please God, please. I am freaking out. Please help
me." I pulled myself together as much as I could and got ready. I grabbed

my bass to leave, all while praying under my breath. Just as I was exiting my house, my phone began to ring. I hadn't been expecting much of a miracle this late in the situation. It was my bass professor on the phone. He told me very casually that, due to a scheduling conflict, my audition had to be canceled. Just those words brought such a relief, but that wasn't all. He went on to say that because of the tight schedule that all the professors had, they were going to let me into the music school without having to audition. I kept my composure long enough to thank my professor for the good news. But after we hung up, I burst into tears. Tears of joy, of pure relief, and of thankfulness streamed down my cheeks. I sat on my front steps, thanking God. He saw me in my time of need and met me where I was at. My problem wasn't too small or insignificant to Him.

God sees us in every instance of our lives, and He cares about what we care about. When we can't see the outcome or the reason for the madness we're experiencing, God makes a way to shine His goodness and mercy over all these aspects of our lives. Trust in Him because He truly cares for you and can always make a way.

FATHER, GUIDE MY SWORD
by Becky Blanchard

"See, I am doing a new thing! Now it springs up; do
you not perceive it? I am making a way in the wilderness
and streams in the wasteland."

Isaiah 43:19 (NIV)

"He reveals deep and hidden things; he knows what
lies in darkness, and light dwells with Him."

Daniel 2:22 (NIV)

If you've seen the movie "The Princess Bride," you'll get this devo
title. In one scene of the movie, this guy was in a forest holding up his
father's sword needing to find a place that was hidden somewhere un-
derground. He closed his eyes and said, "Father, guide my sword." He
pointed the sword out, and with his eyes closed, stumbled a few steps
and found it—the secret passageway. That was us in Bali a few years ago.
And in life, you're not always going to know the way. Sometimes it's just
like us stepping out blindly, asking and trusting God to guide you. You
know what needs to happen, but the 'who,' 'where,' and 'how's' can still
be a blur.

When we first arrived in Bali, God really confirmed the place where
we were to start with the kids on the streets in the main tourist area.
These kids (from ages 6-15 years old) would spend their evenings well
into late hours like 4-5 AM, walking the streets where the most popular
bars and nightclubs are. All night long they try to sell bracelets to the
tourists there. We met the kids weekly, giving them opportunities just
to be kids and play games—not having to worry about selling or making
a certain quota to support their family for that hour. We'd also share
food with them and spend time telling them about our good friend Jesus. Over time, after we started building relationships with them, we got
to hear their stories and found that almost all were originally from this
one village in North Bali—known as one of the poorest regions in Bali's
poorest region. The mothers and their kids had moved down to the
south of Bali to sell bracelets, beg in streets, or work at massage parlors.

We realized, even though the things we were doing with them were

Faith Food Devotional

good, it wouldn't be enough to fix the problem of them having to be there all night working in such horrible places for children. So much of what they were seeing every day was having an impact on them, and they were even victims of many cases of abuse from those under the influence of drugs and alcohol. There was a major problem, and we were just scratching the surface. We learned that this had been a life cycle for generations for these families coming from that village. To make any significant difference, we needed to go to the source and start to work there as well.

44

We only knew the name of the village they were from but didn't know anyone there or have any exact addresses. So as a team, we decided to go on a scouting trip. We piled in a car together, put the name of the village in Google Maps, prayed that God would guide us and drove North! We had developed a ministry program called Aslan's Sidewalk Academy that has educational components to it, and we took with us a brochure folder we had made. The plan was to show it to any village leader or anyone that worked at a school once we arrived. We finally reached a sign with the village name on it and we all cheered. We made it! Then we looked at each other and laughed—now what? As we kept driving, we looked for any official-like buildings or anything that resembled a school. Finally one of our team members said, "Hey, look, that wall has the word 'school' painted on it. Let's go check it out." Long story short, we pulled over and met a guy that was there, but found out that the building wasn't even a school; the wall in front of the home was just advertising the school. This however began a very significant conversation and relationship with this man. After we shared our heart and the brochure, he was so touched that he called his uncle who was one of the village leaders. Before you knew it, we were invited to the chief village leader's house for tea that afternoon to share more! We were given permission to use a building there to set up our kids' center and have been there ever since, sharing God's love and light! We later found out that this area had been so strongly set in their Hindu traditions that, 12 years earlier, when local pastors went to try to set something up, they were chased out with stones! Thankfully we've had peace and favor with the community, and have been bringing the most important kind of peace of all to them—peace with God through Jesus!

The point of the story is that sometimes you find yourself in a place where there is a need, but you have no idea where to start. Just because you don't know where to start or what to do, regardless of how far back or deep the issues might be, doesn't mean you shouldn't step out and begin somewhere. You are part of the solution! It's taking that first step, praying and trusting God—that was exactly what led us to where we needed to be and where we are today. God knows the way and He assures us that He will make a way even in the places we don't see one.

PRAY WITHOUT CEASING

by Ismael Garza

> "Pray without ceasing."
>
> 1 Thessalonians 5:17 (ESV)

My family and I went through a difficult moment when my dad decided to leave home and asked my mom for a divorce. This was one of the most difficult seasons that my family went through. At that time, my family was also far from God. We were Christians but never had a real relationship with God. We only knew Him as a religion. My brother and I used to party, drink a lot, and we did drugs.

This all started affecting my mother, and she started going back to church. That is when my mother encountered Jesus. Little by little, my mother began to pray for our own encounters with Jesus. After 6 months of her faithfully praying for us as a family, my brother started to come back to Jesus, and I followed after 7 months. My mom, brother and I started serving God in church together. We got baptized, and each began a personal relationship with God. It definitely was an exciting time, but Jesus wasn't finished yet!

Two years later, we were still going to church, but my dad wasn't. He was in a relationship with another woman. At that point, I couldn't see my dad ever coming back home to us. My mom continued to pray and trust Jesus for my dad's life. My mother kept praying as God had given her a promise that my dad was going to return home. It was so hard for me to believe that. She never stopped praying. After 3 years, God ANSWERED her prayers. My dad had a personal encounter with Jesus that led him to come back home. The best part of it all is that today my dad is a pastor for a church of 100 people, my brother is the worship leader, and I'm a missionary.

Today, I want to encourage you to never give up on whatever promises God has given you and will give in the future! Never stop praying! No matter the situation, or the circumstances, God is working. He hears your prayers and His timing is perfect. His plans are good and He will do what He promised. His plans are way better than what you can imagine. Do you trust Him today? Then pray without giving up!

46

WINGS INTERNATIONAL

FAITH CAN MAKE YOU WELL
by David Blanchard

"And he said to her, 'Daughter, your faith has made
you well; go in peace and be healed of your affliction.'"
Mark 5:34 (NASB)

Mark 5:21-42 tells the story of two healings that took place by people putting their faith in the all-powerful, all-knowing, and omnipresent God. The second story is about a woman who had been hemorrhaging for twelve years and had spent all of her money on the physicians who had tried to make her better but could not. She believed that if she could just touch Jesus, she would be better. Then one day she saw Jesus and touched his clothes and was immediately healed of her affliction. Jesus said that her faith had made her whole!

47

One time in Cuba, I was asked to preach in a church in Matanzas. I was outside praying in the Spirit during the usual one-hour worship service. I was going to preach on faith. When I went into the side door of the church, I was at the front of the building by the worship team and I saw the people totally worshiping God with all of their hearts. God's Spirit said to me, "I want you to call the sick forward before you preach." I said, "God, I need to preach on faith before I pray for the people so that they will receive their healing." God said, "Call the sick forward to be healed." I had a one-on-one discussion with the Holy Spirit to try to help him understand that they needed faith before they could be healed. Then he said to me, "Hey, who is the healer, you or me?" I replied, "Lord, you are the healer!" I heard again, "Then call the sick forward." When I asked if those needing prayer for healing would please come forward, I expected four or five sick people to step up, but about forty-five people came down to the front! Wow! You see, there is no medicine in Cuba that is available for the common citizen. It is only available for government workers. The doctors do all that they can at the clinics and local hospitals and literally say, "Sorry, we can't do anymore. But if you want to, you can try to go over to that church where they pray for people and maybe something will happen." One lady that came forward in the church service was a doctor at the local hospital. She had worked there for about six years. She told me that for the last year and a half she had been hemorrhaging and all of the doctors in the hospital had tried to help her, but she only got worse. I told her about the woman in the Bible who had the same problem for twelve years; she spent all of her money on the doctors and on medicine and only got worse. But one day, she touched Jesus and was totally cured. I asked the doctor, "Do you believe that God can heal you?" She said that she did and then I laid my hands on her shoulders. I said, "In Jesus' name, receive your healing!" She went straight back on the floor. I did not push her. The healing power of God came on her. I was then greatly encouraged and I preached on faith.

48

When we put our faith in God and are in His presence, there's everything that you need. He inhabits the praises of his people. When God's presence is there, all that you need, and more, is available: salvation, forgiveness, restoration, healing, provision, strength, and peace. When we worship the true God with everything we have, everything he has becomes accessible to us. When I arrived back to the USA after the trip, the Cuban pastor called me to see if I had arrived OK. He found out that I had been interrogated. He said, "Hey, did you hear what happened to the doctor lady?" I said, "I guess God healed her." He told me that she believed God had healed her, and the next day she woke up totally healed! She told all the doctors who didn't believe her until after she had a medical examination. Even the atheistic doctors said that surely there must be a God in heaven! The Cuban pastor said, "Brother David, we are now having revival at the church!" Praise God!

All throughout the Bible, we read stories about people who put their faith in God. "Faith shows the reality of what we hope for; it is the evidence of things we cannot see." Hebrews 11:1 (NLT)

Hebrews 11:6 says that, "Without faith it is impossible to please God." We must believe in the invisible, almighty God to see visible results. If you want to see something that you have never seen before, you have to do something that you have never done before. You must believe in the Almighty God who can bring restoration, peace, love, and healing in your life and in the life of those around you. Your faith can make you whole!

THE TOY RIFLE
by Ricardo Rayon

"You can ask for anything in my name, and I will do
it, so that the Son can bring glory to the Father. Yes, ask
me for anything in my name, and I will do it!"
John 14:13-14 (NLT)

"So if you sinful people know how to give good gifts
to your children, how much more will your heavenly
Father give good gifts to those who ask Him."
Matthew 7:7-11 (NLT)

I have an older brother, and when we were kids, he had a toy rifle
that nobody could touch. It was his favorite toy. He still has that toy up
until this very day. One day while I was at my dad's house in Mexico, my
nephew (my brother's son) found the toy rifle. My brother wasn't there,
and I knew how much he liked that rifle, but my nephew wanted that
toy. I told him, "Let's call your dad and ask if you can play with that toy."
I called my brother and my nephew asked for the toy rifle. My brother
responded that yes, he could have it. At that moment my nephew began
to shout, "I knew it, I knew it!" I asked him, "What did you know?" He
said, "I knew my dad would give me that toy because he is my dad, and
he loves me."

That small revelation hit me! God always answers our prayers because He is a good father. He fulfills the desires of the heart. We just
need to ask, and He will answer. We can have the assurance that He
listens to our prayers, and when we believe and trust Him, He will do it!

When you seek the Kingdom of God and His justice, everything else
comes and will be added to you. I remember when I prayed for my first
car, and God provided the car I wanted. Even with my need for a laptop,
or my desire to go to the Taj Mahal in India, I knew my God would provide. He is not a genie in a bottle that gives you everything you want,
but rather He is the one who provides for you more than you need.

Let's take a moment to thank God for His goodness. He is your good
father, He loves you, and He is with you. When we ask and pray in Jesus'
name, our Father in heaven will be glorified through the Son.

Faith Food Devotional

ASK HIM
by Becca Giles

"Keep on asking, and you will receive what you ask for. Keep on seeking, and you will find. Keep on knocking, and the door will be opened to you. For everyone who asks, receives. Everyone who seeks finds. And to everyone who knocks, the door will be opened. You parents—if your children ask for a loaf of bread, do you give them a stone instead? Or if they ask for a fish, do you give them a snake? Of course not! So if you sinful people know how to give good gifts to your children, how much more will your heavenly Father give good gifts to those who ask Him."

Matthew 7:7-11 (NLT)

After God unquestionably confirmed to me to move to Asia, I was now faced with the biggest amount of financial provision I'd ever needed. This amount of money that I had to raise was, to me, seemingly impossible at the time. I cleaned houses for a living. I didn't quite know where to begin, so I got alone, I walked, I prayed, and I asked every day.. for thousands of dollars. Reaching people was and will always be my motive, and God knows that. Greed was not a factor. I was only doing what I knew Jesus says I should do (Matthew 21:22, John 15:16).

During this season of fundraising, I had a dream at night where my pastor handed me a check that was made out for US$120. In the dream, he and his wife prophesied over me saying, "This money is going to multiply to the full amount that you need." I woke up, wrote down my dream, and went to class at the ministry school I was attending.

My pastor (the same pastor as in the dream I'd just had) came up to me and told me he had sold his beloved fishing gear to give me the money he'd made from it. He gave me a chunk of cash and I thanked him, hugged him, and went home. Later that afternoon, I opened my purse and took out the money to count it. It was all $20 bills. I counted..20, 40, 60, 80, 100, 120...I almost had a heart attack. The same man who gave me $120 dollars in my dream the night before just gave me the same amount in real life. The dream came to pass, and within a short time period through the unselfish, wild generosity of the Body of Christ, God provided the entire "impossible" amount that I needed—and even more.

God isn't a vending machine for you to come to and get anything you want, but He is not teasing when He tells you to ask Him for what you need.

Don't let worry and complaining make any space for itself in your heart for even a second. Be specific, and ask Him. Keep on asking, and trust that He will do it. You have permission to do what His Word says.

Take a moment. The King of the Universe is attentive to your need, and He is the best Father who intends to give you a good gift and to give you His Kingdom. You can ask God about endless things—not just for financial provision. What are you dreaming for the future? What's happening in your daily life that needs some God-intervention? What ungodly thought patterns need to bow down to His feet?

Whatever it is that's on your heart, ask God about it—don't forget the details. He catches every word and does not neglect those who seek Him.

51

DELIVERANCE
by Taryon Crawford

> "The Spirit of the Lord is on me, because he has
> anointed me to proclaim good news to the poor. He
> has sent me to proclaim freedom for the prisoners and
> recovery of sight for the blind, to set the oppressed free."
> Luke 4:18 (NIV)

I have prayed for freedom and deliverance for people in the past, but while living and ministering in Africa, I had not yet experienced this level of demonic oppression amongst people before. As believers, because Jesus overcame death, hell, and the grave through His death, burial, and resurrection, we also have overcome all works of darkness.

Our team was able to minister in a remote village of Mozambique because two village leaders had heard the Gospel a week before and wanted their villagers to experience Christ as they had. After showing the Jesus Film, we created something called a "fire tunnel", which is where two lines of people are formed so that others can walk through it and receive prayer. As I was ministering with another lady on my team, a young woman came through our part of the line and had such an evil stare. As we continued to pray, it was quite obvious that she was being heavily oppressed by Satan. The Holy Spirit gave us the words to pray, and we stayed with her for almost an hour until her face, eyes, and body looked normal again. She encountered Jesus and had felt freedom and peace for the first time in years.

One of my favorite stories in the Bible is when Jesus brings His disciples to a remote place and finds a demon-possessed man tied up in chains. Jesus went there for this man to experience God's love, and be set free from the evil one. Today our call is the same, and we need not be afraid. Know that Christ in you is the Deliverer. When we pray for others who are wrongfully tied up in the chains of the enemy, many will be set free in Jesus' name.

DREAM INTERPRETATION 101
by Donna Blanchard

"For God does speak—now one way, now another—
though no one perceives it. In a dream, in a vision of the
night, when deep sleep falls on people as they slumber
in their beds, He may speak in their ears and terrify
them with warnings, to turn them from wrongdoing and
keep them from pride, to preserve them from the pit,
their lives from perishing by the sword."

Job 33:14-18 (NIV)

53

Dreams. How important are they? It says in Acts 2:17 that in the last days we will dream dreams. In the Bible, dreams are seen everywhere and they bring the light of what God is doing in each situation and how He wants to make things known to us. What is the difference between a dream and a vision? Dreams happen when you are sleeping, visions are when you are wide awake.

Dreams from your own creative mind are usually filled with activities from the day, or they are simply interesting. Sometimes, what we eat can cause unusual dreams. But, if you want dreams from the Lord, just ask Him to reveal Himself in your dreams.

Now, dreams from the Lord are all throughout the Bible. Many times, we read right over them and we don't see the great evil avoided by paying attention to a dream. For example, Jesus' earthly father, Joseph, was put in charge of the son of God on this earth as one who was to care for, provide for, and protect. When Jesus was very small (about 1 1/2 to 2 years old), Joseph was warned in a dream to get up immediately and take the child, Jesus, and his mother to escape to Egypt. What would have happened if Joseph thought to himself, "Well that is a strange dream, but it's the middle of the night so I will just wait until morning." He could have said there was no rational reason to leave because they were doing well here. But he was an obedient man. Not much is said of him other than that he was a man who obeyed immediately. Once the situation in Bethlehem was no longer any threat, Joseph was once again given insight by a dream that it was time to leave Egypt and go to the homeland of Israel.

Now if you receive a literal dream and it is not good, like someone dies, or you dream about an accident, God could be revealing to you what the devil has planned. The dream is so you can counterattack the enemy and cancel his plans for destruction through prayer. In our years in the ministry we have had many such dreams and have learned we must always act immediately. There have been many occasions we have successfully stopped the enemies plans with no loss of life!

54

Dreams can warn, dreams can instruct, and sometimes dreams are literal. Dreams can also be full of symbolism. There are dreams with hidden meanings, which means that they are not so clear; you remember them vividly, but just on the surface they don't make sense. The Holy Spirit is one who will help you decipher the clue. These dreams are very helpful with how to pray for future events, and they can even be for direction. They're also great sources of hope.

Sometimes the interpretations do not come overnight. The Holy Spirit will help you every step of the way. Keep seeking, asking, and search it out. God conceals things to draw us closer as we search it out. Once you have the interpretation, you can pray in a correct way and declare the will of God in that situation. Proverbs 25:2 says, "It is the glory of God to conceal a matter, but the glory of kings is to search out a matter." God wants to speak to you in your dreams; ask Him to reveal Himself to you while you sleep.

FISHER OF MEN
by Ismael Garza

> "And he said to them, 'Follow me, and I will make
> you fishers of men.'"
>> Matthew 4:19 (NASB)

I remember when I was 18 years old, I loved to go to church and serve in the media team, especially being behind the camera. I also enjoyed hearing the stories from the missionaries that came to visit my church. A strong desire was birthed in my heart during that time in my life to serve God, but I didn't know anything about what it meant to be a missionary. All I knew was that I enjoyed serving God at church and desired to do that for the rest of my life. When I look back now, I know God was preparing me and calling me. The day I responded to His call was when I was brought to my knees. It was that day that I surrendered myself to His plans for me, and I asked Him to keep me in His will, no matter what life was going to throw at me.

At age 28, a friend invited me to pray to join him to be part of the Wings International missionary team that he worked with in Asia. I didn't tell anyone, but I only prayed about it. After two days of prayer, a friend of mine had a dream that confirmed God's purpose for me to move there to be a part of Wings. It took 10 years of being shaped and prepared for the call that Jesus stirred in my heart at age 18 until that moment. This journey has not been easy, but when it gets tough I always go back to that moment when I surrendered my life to Jesus at 18 years old.

This devotion might be speaking to two groups of people. One group of you may be feeling the tug in your heart that God is calling you to something, but you don't know what he's called you too. I encourage you to pray and ask God why He is stirring something in your heart. The second group of you may already know that God has called you to serve Him. I would encourage you to ask God to confirm where He wants you, and when to start. Then, wait for Him to show you, just like He did with me.

The call that Jesus has over your life doesn't necessarily mean that He is calling you to go to another nation. It could be as simple as talking to someone in your workplace, reaching out to your neighbor, starting a ministry in your church for widows, single people, children, or the youth. If you feel fear, anxiety, or impatience, just go back to the moments when Jesus spoke to you. Remember the time you gave your life to Him, and find His truth that you can hold on to.

PRESSING ON TOWARD THE GOAL
by Rob Giles

"I press on toward the goal to win the prize for which
God has called me heavenward in Christ Jesus."
Philippians 3:14 (NIV)

I was never very competitive when I was little, but in my teen years, I started to play organized sports more frequently in school. During these years I learned the importance of hard work and discipline so that I could become better at the sport I was playing. The goal, of course, was so that as an individual, or as part of a team, we would win a prize.

Many people are driven in their lives this way because they feel a need to succeed, even though the effort and discipline put into achieving these goals can be quite demanding. There's a level of satisfaction that we feel when we know we have given our very best to win that 'prize' that is before us. There's satisfaction in reflecting on all that was done to accomplish this goal: the work, discipline and effort put into it; knowing in the end that it was worth it. When we live out our lives before the Lord, our prize awaiting us is heaven and eternity. That thought excites me!

Even though you may face hardships and trials in this life, continue to press on toward the call that Jesus has placed on you to follow Him. Whatever it takes, I want to achieve that goal. I know for certain that in the end, it will all be worth it.

What about you? What kind of prize are you trying to win?

HELLO HURRICANE
by Becky Blanchard

"And we know that God causes everything to work
together for the good of those who love God and are
called according to His purpose for them... Can anything ever separate us from Christ's love? Does it mean
he no longer loves us if we have trouble or calamity, or
are persecuted, or hungry, or destitute, or in danger, or
threatened with death? (As the Scriptures say, 'For your
sake we are killed every day; we are being slaughtered
like sheep.') No, despite all these things, overwhelming
victory is ours through Christ, who loved us."

Romans 8:28, 35-37 (NLT)

"I have told you these things, so that in me you may
have peace. In this world you will have trouble. But take
heart! I have overcome the world."

John 16:33 (NIV)

'Hello Hurricane' is a song and album title by the band Switchfoot
and the year it was released, all of the songs seemed so significant to
me, especially this one. I have gone through various difficulties in my
life, as everyone does, but nothing could compare to the 2002 Mexico
van accident I was in. I was with a team of youth and staff who were
working with my parent's ministry. It was an amazing trip to one of my
most favorite cities in the world, Mexico City. Thousands had received
Christ during that trip. We were only 3 hours away from arriving back to
our base at the Mexico-Texas border. It was nighttime, and all of a sudden, the back tire blew out and caused the van to roll over three times
on the highway. Three team members were thrown out onto the road,
including myself. The other two were seventeen-year-old girls, and sadly they both lost their lives that day.

One more member in the front passenger seat also died. It was the
hardest and most horrific moment of all our lives. The ambulance took
me to the worst hospital in the city because they were certain I was going to die. That's what they told my sister in the ambulance. She refused

to believe it and said, "No! She's my best friend and you don't know my God. He can do a miracle!" and she started to pray for me.

In short, I lost a lot of blood because of a ruptured spleen, and I broke my jaw and fractured it on the other side. I broke my ribs, the skin on my forehead had been cut open badly, and doctors found 9 blood spots on my brain. They explained that this meant permanent brain damage. It didn't look good. The doctors told my parents that if I lived, I would not be the same Becky. They now would need to hire a nurse to bathe me, dress me, and feed me. I would need to stay in intensive care for two months and regular hospital care for six months, and therapy for two years. My parents politely replied to these doctors, "Well, thank you, but we're also believing another report." "What other report? What other doctor are you seeing?" they responded. "His name is Jesus," my parents replied. "Oh, you're one of those people. Well, we're just telling you the facts." My parents thanked them for doing their job, but they also believed in a God who worked miracles—so they were going to believe for a miracle. In that moment, my parents decided they would put God's truth above facts.

They kept speaking the word of God over me as they prayed for me and had many others join in as well. Miraculously one morning, the nurse walked in and I was sitting up in bed, conscious and talking. The nurses were amazed and exclaimed how it was a miracle. I was released from the hospital only after seventeen days. When I went back a couple of months later for another MRI brain scan, the doctors said, "This is impossible. She used to have 9 blood spots and those don't go away. There is not one trace of a blood spot in her brain." They continued, "This is what medical science calls impossible, this is what you Christians call a miracle!" I'm here today because I have experienced first-hand the miraculous-healing power of God, alive and still active!

But what about those others who lost their lives? And why did this even happen to us in the first place? We were all doing God's will. Was it because of a lack of faith or not praying enough? Was it the devil? Was it God? I heard everybody inform me of what they thought the reasons were. But seriously, why do bad things happen to good people? Where is God in all of this?

What I learned from this situation is that, in the storms of life, the answer is not so much in understanding the why's. No matter what we go through, the most important factor for us to hold onto is that God is

VERY PRESENT to help us (Psalm 46:1). He is always good (James 1:17). The truth is, since the day that Adam and Eve gave in to Satan, we've lived in a fallen world where sin and evil entered and gained access to all facets of creation. We're in an unjust world where bad things constantly happen to good people. We have to remember that it's always the enemy's plan to steal, kill and destroy (John 10:10); BUT that's why God sent Jesus to bring restoration to that which was stolen and lost in the fall.

60   Despite what we don't understand, we can fully believe and trust in God's goodness. He doesn't bring calamity to us, but He does promise to "work all things together" for our good. He always has the upper hand. We have that promise that He can and will turn bad things that are thrown our way into good; whether it was caused by something outside our control, or sometimes even the bad that happens to us as consequence from our own mess-ups. He is full of mercy when we turn to Him in our brokenness.

So when you find yourself in the middle of a hurricane:

Don't stop believing God's word.

Don't stop believing in miracles.

Don't stop believing His promises.

God is FAITHFUL, He is with you,

and who He is doesn't change!

VALUE
by Taryon Crawford

"So God created man in His own image, in the image of God he created him; male and female he created them."

Genesis 1:27 (ESV)

I remember the first time I became aware that I was being influenced by a lie concerning my value. Because I had experienced sexual abuse from a young age, I really struggled to believe that people had my best interest in mind, much less God. Even though I had a radical encounter with the Holy Spirit at age 18 where I gave my heart and turned to follow Jesus, this area of believing my value has been somewhat of a challenging journey.

At a prayer meeting in my 20's, each person in the meeting wrote their name on a piece of paper, and the other members of the group had to anonymously write what they felt God was speaking over each name. When I read mine it said, "You are precious to God, He fights for you!" This phrase made me cry, because at that time, I honestly did not believe (based on my circumstances) that I was worth fighting for. God used this phrase to give me revelation of my value. The Holy Spirit began ministering deeply to me in this area. He said, "Taryon, Jesus paid a high price for your value. That is not something to take lightly." The understanding that my value was paid for on the cross opened my eyes that I didn't have to hang my head in shame because of my past anymore. Progressively, God showed me that Jesus died for all humanity so we would be restored to the inherent value that He had always intended when He thought of us and created us.

Sometimes still today the lie that I am not valuable can try to creep in based on how others treat me at times. But, God made us beautiful and perfect for Himself and no one can add value to you nor take it away because our value comes from Him. When we know how loved, cared for, and valuable we are to God because of Christ, we can share and show value to others that may not understand how valuable they are.

THE BOY AT THE BEACH
by Stephen Walter

> "I will seek the lost, bring back the scattered, bind
> up the broken and strengthen the sick."
>
> Ezekiel 34:16b (ESV)

> "For the Son of Man has come to seek and to save
> that which was lost."
>
> Luke 19:10 (NASB)

Once in Bali, our ministry site was set up on the beach, and we began to invite anyone around us in the surrounding area. Only a small crowd of 10 or so gathered, but our mission team began our main Gospel drama anyway. Although there weren't many people watching, a warm sensation began to arise from within, almost a giddiness of expectation, and I knew the presence of God was on that beach. As the drama concluded, a student from our team stepped forward to explain the drama and to ask if anyone wanted prayer. The few people who remained cautiously raised their hands and we all spread out to meet them. There was a group of three Muslim boys in their late teens who were on vacation from another island and just happened to be walking by our dramas that evening. Although they didn't speak very much English, they explained that they felt drawn to stay and watch.

One of the boys kept pointing to his heart saying that he could feel something. I knew he was feeling the love of God and asked if he wanted prayer. He immediately said yes, so I gently placed my hand on his shoulder to pray. I began asking God to show this boy his love for him, and just as those words exited my mouth, the boy fell to his knees in tears. I bent down with him as I continued to pray. He was sobbing uncontrollably, all the time pointing to his heart and repeating, "I can feel it! I can feel it!" We knelt there in the sand as he experienced the love of God. As he calmed down and regained his composure, I explained what he had just felt. He kept saying how happy he was to be at the beach that day and how this was no coincidence that we met. Even though this ministry site had the least amount of people in attendance so far on our entire mission trip, God showed up in a mighty way. I couldn't help but think that this whole evening was orchestrated just so that one boy could experience the true love of the Father.

Just as one could walk down the beach and notice a single shell that stands out amongst the rest, God saw that boy amongst all the other people and said, "That one. That's the one I want." It doesn't mean He rejects all the others, but this boy was the one God had left the ninety-nine to seek out, at that time. God has a plan to bring all into His kingdom, even if it means one at a time.

THE QUESTION
by Ricardo Rayon

"Then Jesus said, 'Come to me, all of you who are
weary and carry heavy burdens, and I will give you rest.
Take my yoke upon you. Let me teach you, because I am
humble and gentle at heart, and you will find rest for
your souls. For my yoke is easy to bear, and the burden I
give you is light.'"

Matthew 11:28-30 (NLT)

64

I've been in the ministry for many years. Sometimes I love it, and other days I'm like... "What am I doing here?" In Bali, after a few years of doing kids' ministry, loving them, supporting them, praying for, and being with them, it was difficult for me to see the change in these kids. I had a season where I was wondering, "What am I doing here?"

As I was walking to the beach for our kids'' program one Wednesday night, I was complaining to God, wondering what I was doing there. The night went as usual, but at the end, one of the teenage girls who regularly came to our program had a diva moment and argued with one of our teachers.

In a begging-tired tone I said to her, "Please respect your teacher." She blew up! She started screaming and cursing. As I saw her there, my heart broke and I felt so much pain. She yelled, "Pepino, I'm mad, I'm angry!" And she cried. I cried too as I felt her pain. I felt how badly she was being abused and my heart was so broken. I apologized in the name of her parents, siblings, foreigners, and any men that had hurt her. We prayed and I felt the Holy Spirit bring peace to her. She hugged me and left. Meanwhile, I cried for another hour.

That night, God showed me why I was there. God broke my heart with the thing that broke His heart. You may feel like me. You may be asking, "What am I doing in this church? What am I doing in my life? What am I doing here?" Or many other questions like that. I want to encourage you to let God break your heart. Let God touch you and drown you in His love and mercy. You can touch other lives, and be Jesus' feet, arms, and words. Your love, and what you say and do, will make a difference.

WHO'S ON YOUR SIDE?
by Ben Lawalata

"...Day after day and night after night they keep on
saying, 'Holy, holy, holy is the Lord God, the Almighty—
the one who always was, who is, and who is still to
come.'"

Revelation 4:8 (NLT)

I remember when I was about 10 years old, I was with some friends one evening after school. That night, we decided to watch a horror film. I came home from the movie feeling absolutely disturbed and scared. My parents weren't home. I couldn't shake off the feeling of being afraid, so I decided to read the Bible. I was merely doing it as a deed. I didn't understand what I was reading, I was just hoping that I would feel better about myself if I just did the deed of reading the Bible.

At that time in my life, I would go to church, I would sit through a service, I understood that my family's religion was Christian, but I hardly read my Bible. That one night I finished the whole book of Revelation. Even though I was clueless about what I just read that night, somehow I was able to convince myself that I just did a good thing and I should be ok. I didn't find comfort by the understanding of the Word, but it was out of fear that I tried to get closer to God just by reading His Word, and He was faithful to meet me where I was. Fear left me, and I was at peace.

A few years later, as I was tuning into some news, I got really discouraged by the thought of how people with power and money have the capacity to bring lives to ruin. Evil things and satanic acts that are happening all around really are displaying the enemy's dominion. I felt overwhelmed and powerless. Again I was disturbed, and fear started to take over. Then God reminded me of the night when I read through the whole book of Revelation. I found myself again fearful, so I picked up my Bible and started reading. This time, however, was different.

Not far into the book, God had me see who He is. In the book of Revelation, just by how His might and splendor is described, I right away understood that this is what He wanted me to know when I was 10—the same way for that very moment. I understood who is on my side, and who I should bow down to. He is the only one to be feared. The Almighty, who is eternal, He is beyond life and death. There is nothing to be feared but God. No matter how many things that are out of my control, He is the one who has power over all things. This is my peace at times of uncertainties and troubles, the magnitude of the God that I worship and bow to is beyond and above everything else.

The best part about all this is not just that He is almighty, and matchless in power; He is also matchless in love, and He is a personal God who desires a relationship with us. Revelation 21:3-4 says "...Look, God's home is now among His people! He will live with them, and they will be His people. God Himself will be with them. He will wipe every tear from their eyes. And there will be no more death or sorrow or crying or pain. All these things are gone forever."

Sometimes we may feel overwhelmed by the things that are out of our power, things that are out of our control. But take heart. God, who is on our side and who is for us, He is still in control. He is bigger than anything, mightier than anyone and any being. So whenever you feel fearful or threatened by the lies of the enemy about his dominion and influence, remember that the Lord God, The Almighty is on your side. The enemy doesn't stand a chance. May this bring peace into your life.

MASTERPIECE
by Becca Giles

"For we are God's masterpiece. He has created us
anew in Christ Jesus, so we can do the good things he
planned for us long ago."

Ephesians 2:10 (NLT)

Enough. You're enough! There's an invisible standard that the world
has declared existence to, that says you must measure up to it to be
good enough; good enough for who? Before you did anything, or looked
like anything, before you were formed inside your mother, you were already enough in the eyes of your Creator. You are His perfectly formed
together, thought-over masterpiece. You're enough to the extent that
the blood of His son Jesus defines the measure of your worth. The blood
of Jesus that makes you wholly enough, and removes any sin that tries
to claim ownership in your life.

Knowing about your identity in Christ is good; but knowing it, keep-
ing it in the forefront of your mind, and choosing to live in the revelation of your identity in Christ is best.

My mom spent so many hours teaching me how to spell when I was
a child. "C A T. That spells 'cat', Becca!" I would sound it out with her
and repeat C A T. Over and over again. I could remember how to spell it
as she taught me, but an hour later I would not be able to spell "cat" for
the life of me if she asked me to. Jesus, bless my mom for her patience.

Hold fast to the revelation God has given you about your identity
in Him—it's good to remind yourself. It's possible to break the cycle of
having to re-learn and believe it over and over again. Yield old thought
patterns, old beliefs, and old habits to His refining fire. Let the Father's
"Enough" spoken over you be what leads you in your thoughts, actions,
and choices today. Every day.

Now, Lord, we declare that you are enough..with nothing else. You
are our purpose. Our life. Bread and water to our souls. You are wisdom.
You are all that we need. You are Father, friend, lover, and savior. Thank
you that we'll never be in lack because you are our Enough.

I WILL FIGHT FOR YOU
by Becky Blanchard

> "The Lord will fight for you, and you have only to be silent."
>
> Exodus 14:14 (ESV)

> "No weapon that is fashioned against you shall succeed, and you shall refute every tongue that rises against you in judgment. This is the heritage of the servants of the Lord and their vindication from me, declares the Lord."
>
> Isaiah 54:17 (ESV)

There was this one time when the Wings team was planning to head to India on a ministry trip. A couple of days before arriving, we were in Nepal and I started receiving email threats from a radical Hindu who did not like Christians at all and had heard that we were coming. He began sending repeated threats to start a riot against us, to chase us out, and deport us back to our home countries. I'm not one to retreat easily, but I also didn't want to be stupid and jeopardize our local partners or my team, so we went to God in prayer. I knew what the email said, I knew how uneasy this made some on my team feel, but what was God saying about this? I asked the Holy Spirit to guide us and what we should do in this situation. Should we go back to our base in Indonesia, or should we move ahead as planned? Things didn't make sense, but for some reason, I still had peace inside. I also sought counsel from our local minister friends, and we all felt the peace of God to move forward. I had asked God to give us a specific scripture to hold onto if it was His will for us to move forward. The next morning, I opened my YouVersion Bible App, and the scripture of the day was Exodus 14:14. "I will fight for you, all you have to do is be silent." I shared it with the team, that was all we needed to hear! That scripture came up a couple more times over the next several days through different social media modes, assuring us of His presence with us. We got to India and had an awesome time of ministry to the children and sharing the gospel in slums to families that had never heard of Jesus before! Everything happened as planned, and on the night that we were waiting to board our flights to return our Indonesia base, I opened the YouVersion app again to see what the verse of the day was. It was Isaiah 54:17: "This is the heritage of the servants of the Lord." C'mon! What a great note to end the trip on!

God is in your corner, guys! He's got your back and is your defender! Always remember, the safest, best place to be is in the center of God's will.

SABAM POLOLU MOUNTAIN EXPERIENCE
by Ria Lowing

"The LORD is my shepherd, I shall not be in want.
He makes me lie down in green pastures; he leads me
beside quiet waters. He restores my soul; he guides me
in paths of righteousness for His name's sake. Even
though I walk through the valley of the shadow of death,
I will fear no evil, for you are with me; your rod and your
staff, they comfort me. You prepare a table before me in
the presence of my enemies; you have anointed my head
with oil; my cup overflows. Surely goodness and lovingkindness will follow me all the days of my life, and I will
dwell in the house of the LORD forever."

Psalm 23:1-6 (NASB)

In 2018, I was with a team visiting more than 15 villages in a remote
area of Sulawesi, Indonesia for a month. When we arrived in a village,
we decided to climb the highest mountain on that island to pray. The
weather was so nice and sunny when we decided to climb the mountain
in the morning. However, while we were on our way, we did not see
the rain that was about to come. The track was so extreme, and there
was a valley to our left and right side. When we arrived at the top of
the mountain, I prayed and read Psalm 23. Not long after reading these
verses, dark clouds showed up and surrounded the place on the peak—
heavy rain was coming. We didn't have any of the necessary equipment
you need for hiking in this kind of condition. As we were heading back
down to the village, we experienced many obstacles with extreme conditions, and one of my friends fell into a hole. Even as the way back
down the mountain was so difficult and dark, my heart felt brave as
I remembered the verses saying not to fear because God is with me. I
witnessed that day how God's help was so real in my team as we arrived
back to the village safely. Jesus saved us from danger.

The Word of God is alive. We have to hold onto it and believe in it.
No matter what your conditions are like right now, believe that God is
your good shepherd—He'll always be with you. He guides us in paths
of righteousness, even when we walk through the valley. He is with us.

GOD IS PURSUING YOU!
by Ismael Garza

> "I will bless you with a future filled with hope—a
> future of success, not of suffering."
>
> Jeremiah 29:11 (CEV)

When I was in bible college, we did a lot of evangelism training around Mexico. We would teach the body of Christ how to pray and how to share the Good News. We would go out with the church to do outreaches on the streets, and one day we had a strategy that we would go out and do a "treasure hunt." A treasure hunt is a way to preach the Gospel through getting words of knowledge for people that we ask Jesus for before we would go out and minister. We want to find God's "treasure," which is people. It was my first time doing something like this. We asked the Holy Spirit for someone's name and the color of the dress or t-shirt of the person that He wanted to encounter that day. I prayed, and God gave me the name Sonia—which is not a common name in Mexico. As soon as we finished waiting on and asking the Holy Spirit for words of knowledge, we went out to find His treasures. After 10 minutes, I decided to ask every lady that walked in front of me if her name was Sonia. In 2 minutes, I found Sonia. She was speechless when I told her how God had given me her name and why I was asking. Sonia had been going through a bad season with her family, and she expressed how she knew Jesus was pursuing her through me talking with her. We prayed together, and she received Jesus that day.

I want to encourage you, as you leave your home today, ask God for a clue: a name, color of clothing, or picture. There is someone today that Jesus wants to encounter. There are so many people that we come across every day that are lost, need love, and need encouragement. Jesus wants to use us to bring them into encounters with Him. We are His voice to these people. When we step out in obedience, it is exciting and we also get to experience God's love and goodness in those moments.

I WANT TO KNOW WHAT LOVE IS
by Rob Giles

"Love is patient, love is kind. It does not envy, it does not boast, it is not proud. It does not dishonor others, it is not self-seeking, it is not easily angered, it keeps no record of wrongs. Love does not delight in evil but rejoices with the truth. It always protects, always trusts, always hopes, always perseveres."

1 Corinthians 13:4-7 (NIV)

Let me give you a brief backstory. The year was 1984. I was just a young adult who didn't really have a full understanding of what love was really all about. During that year, the song 'I Want To Know What Love Is' was written by the band Foreigner. I guess they were thinking they needed to know this answer as well. I'm sure through history several people have undertaken the task of trying to explain what this word 'love' really means too, and many people have their own ideas of what it is.

As a result of my upbringing, I can undoubtedly say that my understanding of love was very confused. My parents divorced when I was only 5, and I had a stepfather who was abusive. I did not understand the kind of bond that a father and son should have while I was growing up. Basically, all the role models I was looking to for answers fell short and left me feeling brokenhearted. After I had asked Jesus to come into my life in 1984, the word 'love' became alive to me. It was hard for me to grasp how Jesus could love me so much that He would be willing to die for me. The 13th chapter of Corinthians is known as the 'Love Chapter,' and I have since spent many years studying it, gaining a wealth of wisdom and understanding. There are still times when I don't practice all that is taught in these verses, but I am grateful that Jesus continually reminds me of the ultimate love and sacrifice He gave for me on the cross. He always leads me to ask for His forgiveness and calls me to express love as it's written in scripture.

What would you say your perception of 'love' is? Have you also had a confused, misunderstood meaning of what it truly is? Look to Jesus for the answers today. You will not be disappointed.

CAN MY TESTIMONY BRING YOU GLORY?
by Chantel Garza

"You intended to harm me, but God intended it for
good to accomplish what is now being done, the saving
of many lives."

Genesis 50:20 (NIV)

We all have a past, right? I don't know if you have ever done something and thought, "How could I ever share this part of life as a testimony?" or "How could what I have done ever bring glory to Jesus?" Well,
I have! I have a past filled with bad choices. A past including a wrong
relationship. These choices brought me into depression and self-hatred.
Because of this, I struggled with the thought of sharing it with others
as my testimony. I wanted to share Jesus' goodness, forgiveness, and
healing in my life, but I didn't want to share what I had done. I realized
in my journey of healing, that the impact of how great Jesus is, and His
love, mercy, and acceptance lays within all of our testimonies. YES, Jesus can use any situation to bring Him glory! We only need to be brave
and unashamed to share it.

The day that I said to Satan, "You see, what you intended for evil in
my life, God has turned it to good," was the day that Jesus led me to a
lady that was about to walk into the same sinful trap as I had done before. As I shared with her what I had done, and what the consequences
were, she listened and chose to run away from the same trap.

This was the day that my testimony was used for His glory. I haven't
stopped sharing it since then.

Let's continue to stand with unashamed hearts, knowing the power
of forgiveness, and bravely declaring what Jesus has done for us. What
Jesus did for you He can do the same for others that are about to or have
done the same as you.

Prayer: Thank you, Jesus, for all you have done in my life. Thank
you for forgiving me, and for pulling me out of the pit and clothing me
with righteousness. Jesus, please lead me to the right people that need
to hear my testimony of your goodness and forgiveness—that they too
would be released from any bondage, shame, and sin. Help me to be
brave and ready to share as you lead me. Amen!

Faith Food Devotional

SEE THE MOON?
by Becky Blanchard

> "When I consider your heavens, the work of your
> fingers, the moon and the stars, which you have set in
> place, what is mankind that you are mindful of them,
> human beings that you care for them? You have made
> them a little lower than the angels and crowned them
> with glory and honor. You made them rulers over the
> works of your hands; you put everything under their
> feet."
>
> Psalms 8:3-6 (NIV)

It was my second year at Bible college and I was completely relying on God for the provision to make it through. During the summer before, I had returned to Mexico to work with my parents' ministry for a couple of months. During that time I was involved in a serious car accident. Without going into all the details, it was a miracle that I lived and was even able to leave the hospital.

After returning home for a couple of months, I felt God's direction to go back for my second year. However, since my body was still in the healing process, the doctors instructed me that I wouldn't be able to drive or have a job for at least five to six months. I prayed about it and spoke to my parents that I felt God leading me to return to finish Bible school. My parents, being missionaries, said they would help me financially with anything they could and we would trust God for the rest. So I went back to school, and for the first few months was walking through a process of physical, emotional, and mental healing from the incident I had just gone through. Soon enough, I had to start paying some school bills and I had some other heavy expenses coming up as well. I had no idea how I was going to pay for them and began to feel worry taking over. I took a walk one night and did the best thing I could think to do at the time— go to McDonald's to get a hot fudge sundae!

As I was walking, I remember talking to God and laying out all of my worries and concerns. Then I heard Him speak to my heart. He asked me, "Becky, you see the moon? Who made the moon?" And as I looked at the moon I said, "Well, you, God." Then He asked me, "Now all of your financial needs and these upcoming fees that are larger for you to handle, are they as big as the moon— if you were to compare them in size?" I replied, "Of course not, the moon is massive compared to them!" He told me, "Then if the moon is the work of my hands, can't I handle these financial needs you have?" Right away I felt peace and my heart lifted. I said, "Yes, you're right, God. Thank you. I believe you can handle it and I trust you with it all." I walked away still not knowing exactly how it was going to happen, but I had an assurance inside and faith to move ahead. Not long after that, my parents received a phone call from a family friend of ours who wanted to help with my school fees and anything else they were able to! I would have enough funds to cover my entire year! I even had friends during that season who would pitch in to help me with anything they could.

Let's not forget how much our God truly cares for us, in every area of our lives! There is nothing too small or too big for Him to handle, he's got us in His hands. The most important thing for us to do in these times is to trust Him and believe. I think it made a difference that, after what God showed me about the moon, I responded with my own heart and mouth, vocalizing a faith response like I did. There's something powerful that happens when you join your heart and your words in faith to God.

TUNE IN
Becca Giles

> "My sheep hear my voice, and I know them, and they
> follow me."
>
> John 10:27 (ESV)

Kawika, a prophetic man and radical lover of Jesus, often trained the Body of Christ about prophetic words of encouragement and words of knowledge at my church. You knew that when Kawika was around, good things were about to happen. When I was a young teenager, and still quite a beginner when it came to operating in the gifts of the Spirit, I couldn't wait to go when I heard that Kawika was hosting a training class for us kids in the youth group. He taught us how we can each hear the voice of God, and explained that we were going to do an exercise together to practice what we had just been learning. We would each need to find a partner in the class, and ask the Holy Spirit for an encouraging word for that person. However, we had to ask God for a word for that partner based on a cartoon character!

Immediately as Kawika said this, I heard the quiet voice of the Holy Spirit say to me, "Tweety Bird." I had really never even watched that show with Tweety Bird. I had no idea how God was going to use that for whoever my partner would be. Over and over I kept hearing it. Kawika finished explaining what we were going to do and said that he would now demonstrate an example for us. In the crowd of all the kids, he called out my name and said, "Becca, I hear the Holy Spirit saying 'Tweety Bird' over you." The word I was just hearing seconds before was for me. The Holy Spirit spoke through Kawika that I was like a songbird, but that I would not only worship the Lord through singing and music. He declared over me that my entire life would be like a song of worship unto Jesus. Kawika can't read minds. He didn't know that the Holy Spirit had just whispered, "Tweety Bird" to me. I encountered the deep reality of God that day. I only positioned myself to hear Him speak, and another brother in Christ did the same.

We are His sheep, we hear His voice, He knows us, and we follow Him. We have the Holy Spirit to guide us to the right person, at the right time, and speak only a word that would matter to them, if we simply tune in and listen. This word spoken over me years ago still moves me today to live, breathe, and do everything unto His name and His glory.

When you make yourself available now (and in every kind of situation) to hear from the Holy Spirit, you're creating a place where you, and the lives of those around you, can experience the reality of God. God has been speaking to people since He created the first human beings. It is not a question of if God is speaking. He is speaking and desires to talk with you. Let the prayer of your heart be, "Help me to recognize when you speak to me." Take a moment to be quiet, and listen. How is 77 He speaking to you today?

DOES GOD WANT TO TALK WITH ME?

Ismael Garza

> "My sheep hear my voice, and I know them, and they
> follow me."
>
> John 10:27 (ASV)

I want to tell you something important. Guess what? God wants to talk with you. He wants to have an intimate relationship with you. When God created Adam and Eve, He created them to have a relationship with Him—and that's the same for you and me.

God created you uniquely, and He didn't create anyone else in the exact same way as He created you. Therefore, the way that He speaks with you is also unique, and cannot be compared to how He speaks with someone else. I believe there's a creative way that God wants to speak with you personally. He is the ultimate creator. Think about how He created the stars, the moon, and even the flowers. God wants to cultivate an even deeper, intimate relationship with you through the unique ways that He can speak with you. He could speak to you through painting, or dancing, or music. I encourage you to discover with God how you can hear Him through a different creative form. He is speaking.

For me, God has spoken through nature. One day, as I was laying down on my back outside, God spoke to me as I was looking at the trees. He spoke to me about how He takes care of us and explained to me how we live in different seasons. One season might bear leaves, and the next season you might see fruit. You can hear Him creatively, and you can hear Him through His Word today. The Bible is the most important place where you can learn His character. You can hear of how He created you and intended you to live. You can know His love for you through His Word.

God wants to talk with you in many ways. There is no formula for how He speaks; He is God. He wants to help you navigate living in this world because He loves you so much. Today, let your relationship with Him grow deeper as you open your heart to hear Him however He wants to speak to you.

NOW YOU SEE IT, NOW YOU DON'T
David Blanchard

"And all things you ask in prayer, believing, you will receive."

Matthew 21:22 (NASB).

One time before the Mexico International Harvesters Institute Bible School began, we had a massive "Day of the Child" outreach as well as evening adult crusades. There were over one thousand children present. We had many games and activities for the children along with teaching them about the love of God and the principles of God's kingdom by which to live. Many children gave their hearts to the Lord Jesus Christ. At the evening crusade for the adults, there was an ex-religious priest from Veracruz, Mexico, who was sharing his story of how he became truly born again and a committed follower of Jesus Christ. The neighboring religious women had their windows open and were listening to the testimony of this ex-religious priest who was saying that in all the years of his service in the religious church, he only had a ritualistic, religious relationship with God. The religious women called the higher officials who said that if we didn't stop the crusade, they would send strong men to come the next day and beat up the ex-religious priest and myself. We put our men from the church around the edge of the tent. Many people came to the crusade that evening, and so did the other men in their pick-up trucks driving around to intimidate us. Although they were ready to fight, we kept on preaching the word of God.

The next day, the religious people sent a young boy with a little card saying that if we didn't stop the crusade they would kill the speaker. That night, we, again, preached the Good News of Jesus Christ. During the healing service, a woman named Guillermina came forward and said she had a tumor in her womb that was going to be removed during the following week. She asked if we could please pray for her. She wanted prayer for the surgery to go well. During the prayer, one of the ladies from the Agape church, Grandma Paula, was praying over her along with the guest speaker, other women, and myself. Paula had laid her hand on her womb and we all prayed. Guillermina began to scream, "Ah, ah, someone is cutting me. Ah, ah, help me I'm bleeding!" Paula checked

Faith Food Devotional

and said, "Guillermina, you're not bleeding and no one is cutting you." There was no sign of blood and we finished praying.

The very next week, Guillermina went to the doctor who did the final x-ray before the surgery. When he came back into the room again, the doctor asked her if she had already gone to the hospital. She said she never went to the hospital. The doctor asked her if she had seen another doctor at another clinic. She said that she hadn't done that either. She asked the doctor why he was asking her all these questions. He replied, "Because, we just did the final x-ray before the surgery, and look, here is the previous x-ray from two weeks ago that shows the tumor, and here is the current x-ray. There is no tumor! It's gone. We don't see it on the x-ray. Where did it go?" Guillermina said, "I don't know. I guess God must have healed me last week at the tent crusade!" Praise the Lord! Our faith in God and in his word came together with the faith of Guillermina. God did the impossible for us, which is simply possible for him.

Abraham in the Old Testament was promised to be the father of a nation, the father of multitudes of people. It was said that the number of his children would be like looking up to the multitude of stars in the night sky. The problem was that his wife, Sarah, was barren and they could not have children. Just like God created the world that previously did not exist, so Abraham believed until the very end that he was going to be the father of many people. As the scripture says, "'I have made you a father of many nations.' So the promise is good in the sight of God, in whom Abraham believed—the God who brings the dead to life and whose command brings into being what did not exist." Romans 4:17

We too must believe for those things that we don't see or have. We must believe that God is great enough to do the impossible. What is impossible for man is a simple possibility for the omniscient and omnipotent God who created the universe with all the galaxies, all the planets, and all the stars. We must believe that all things are possible through Christ who strengthens us. We must believe that we will receive all things that we ask in prayer from God. We must believe that God is able to answer our requests. We must trust God and thank him for the answer by faith, even as Abraham faithfully did all his life.

THE BUILDER'S HEART
Ben Lawalata

"Anyone who listens to my teaching and follows it
is wise, like a person who builds a house on solid rock.
Though the rain comes in torrents and the floodwaters
rise and the winds beat against that house, it won't
collapse because it is built on bedrock."

Matthew 7:24-25 (NLT)

I'm not a builder. I may know a thing or two about it, but I hardly have any experience building. But, I know that when we build, we would want to have the right things and ways to do it with. We would also never like to undo our progress. That would feel like taking a backward step from our goals. Here, Jesus says that following Him is like a house that's built right. Not just a building—but our lives, our work, our projects.

About four years ago God called me to Bali. The islanders have their cultural and spiritual beliefs. It's displayed all across the island through statues, shrines, and temples. One night when some friends and I gathered to pray, God gave me a vision of the locals tearing down a shrine. He showed me their dusty, dirty hands and said to me, "What the builders have built will be undone by the same hands. Their hearts will not be for the things they were before." Psalm 118:22-24 says, "The stone that the builders rejected has now become the cornerstone. This is the Lord's doing, and it is wonderful to see. This is the day the Lord has made. We will rejoice and be glad in it."

In the grand scheme of it, yes, revival amongst the islanders! But also, in my personal life and my daily walk is this understanding that there is at times a process of God undoing things in me that aren't what He wants. In those times it may feel like defeat. Turning around is hard because it's admitting error. No one really likes being wrong. Yet, what also happens is that the heart has a new projection. Accepting that you've been wrong feels like defeat, but there's a victory inside when you can surrender this to God. You've been won over by the merciful, good, and generous God.

For Bali, I'm believing for this revival to happen, and it won't be with the anguish of defeat. No, there will be joy as they unbuild their temples

Faith Food Devotional

and idols because God and His truth have got a hold of them. The hearts have turned. They have become His temple.

For us though, at times yes, we have to undo what we think is progress. Sometimes that means turning around and leaving things behind. Hebrews 11:10 says, "Abraham was confidently looking forward to a city with eternal foundations, a city designed and built by God." Let's be confident in the Builder's heart for us in each season, let Him undo what needs to be undone, and let Him build up what He wants to according to His plan.

ALL THAT YOU DO
Rob Giles

"And whatever you do or say, do it as a representative of the Lord Jesus, giving thanks through Him to God
the Father."
Colossians 3:17 (NLT)

Have you ever asked yourself why you do the things that you do? In
the world today, most people have a desire to fill some kind of need or
want that they have in life. It could be for selfish reasons, simple gratifi-
cation, or maybe they just want to please somebody. Many people have
a mindset that they only need to look out for themselves without giving
consideration to others. But if I am, however, a believer and follower of
Christ (which I am), I want to be sure of the reason why I do the things
that I do. As it says in Colossians 3:17, the main reason for anything I
do, or will do, is to bring glory to God. Whatever I do is not really about
me at all—it's all about the Creator of all things. So how do we apply this
to our lives? Let's give thought to this. People will always have a natural
reaction to everything they observe from your life, and your calling is
to simply follow the example of Christ. Do I want to be remembered as
a person who was just looking for a free handout, or as a husband who
was not helpful to his wife, or as a parent who was harsh or cruel to
his children? Our words and actions really do have an impact on those
around us.

I have had several different jobs throughout my life, some of which
I have really enjoyed, and others not so much. There was one particular
job that I just did not like. I had the skill set and qualifications to do
the job well, but this one guy I worked with was really rough around
the edges and had a very crude mouth. It was difficult to be around him
all the time. I was reminded though that I was once just like this, and I
believe God put me in that job just for him. As difficult as it was to work
with him on a daily basis, I knew that if I just surrendered myself to the
Lord, He would receive glory. So that's what I chose to do. Whenever I
had the chance, I would try to speak into his life and be a witness to him.
The more I was around him, the more I noticed slight changes in his
behavior and especially his mouth. I have since moved on from that job,

but I believe the relationship I made with this co-worker had an impact on his life. He calls me regularly and I still take opportunities to share with him about a personal relationship with the Lord. He listens, and I continue to pray for him daily. I know this brings glory to God. I believe someday soon my friend will also have a relationship with Christ.

It says in Romans 1:20, "For since the creation of the world God's invisible qualities, His eternal power and divine nature, have been clearly seen, being understood from what has been made, so that people are without excuse." I find purpose for my life in this knowing that when I am meeting the needs of others, honoring my parents, showing respect to others, expressing kind words or having a peaceful spirit, it's all for the reason of bringing glory to God. This reminder helps me stay focused on living my life as a representative of Jesus, and my prayer is that it will for you as well.

DISCIPLINE BRINGS LOVE & LOVE IS POWERFUL
Donna Blanchard

> "Those who spare the rod of discipline hate their
> children. Those who love their children care enough to
> discipline them."
>
> Proverbs 13:24 (NLT)

When I was a little girl, both sets of my grandparents were alive and I remember both grandmothers in particular. My grandmother on my father's side was very rigid and hard; she had many rules in her house: you sat still in a chair, you did not touch the walls, and you only got up if you were told to. There were toys at her house, but the rules that surrounded them outweighed the joy of playing with them. As a result, we did not play very much with her toys.

My grandmother on my mother's side was very different. Her home was always open, there was plenty of food, plenty of things to do, we were allowed to play everywhere. She had toys, and it was so much fun to play with them with all my cousins. She had a big box of old clothes that she let us girls play with. We would pretend we were princesses going to the ball. There seemed to be no rules—or at least it seemed that way to me compared to my other grandmother.

Then there was my mother; she was the balance between the two extremes. All of my brothers and sisters felt loved, yet at the same time, we were corrected, disciplined, and sometimes the consequences of our decisions came quickly. There seemed to be a healthy balance of good consequences when we did the right thing and we saw (and sometimes felt) the results of our poor choices. My mother was also very consistent in raising us to see down the road and with a long-term consequence perspective of our short-term decisions. Because of that, we were able to make good choices.

The verse above talks about the "rod of discipline," that can be referred to as showing your children accountability, boundaries. In other words, for every action, there is a reaction. Our decisions have consequences; they can be good or bad consequences, but all decisions result in something. Oftentimes our view and perspective of God can be very blurred by our experiences with discipline in our lives or the lack of. On the one hand, my grandmother on my father's side was a very strict authoritative woman. She always came across, in my point of view, as very cold, untouchable, and far away. She seemed only to be concerned with my good behavior and wanting nothing to do with me when I showed bad behavior.

My grandma on my mom's side: full of warmth and compassion, warm hugs, and every square inch of her home was open for all of her grandchildren, made it seem that there were no boundaries. It seemed I could ask her for anything and I would get it. In contrast to my other grandma who believed children are to be seen and not heard. Both of these examples of authority in my life could very easily have warped my thinking.

I believe God would like us to have a healthy balance of both discipline and love; the kind I received from my mother. When the Bible talks about sparing the rod, it is referring to not letting our children follow their fallen nature, but teaching them that each decision they make has consequences and they need to think before they make a decision.

Leaving out the uncomfortableness of discipline will only destroy you in the end. We are God's child and He too will have to discipline us from time to time, but it will always be a balance of both discipline and love. Discipline helps us mature, and love is a powerful force that can change the world for the good!

FORGIVENESS
Taryon Crawford

"Going under the water was a burial of your old life;
coming up out of it was a resurrection, God raising you
from the dead as he did Christ. When you were stuck in
your old sin-dead life, you were incapable of responding
to God. God brought you alive—right along with Christ!
Think of it! All sins forgiven, the slate wiped clean, that
old arrest warrant canceled and nailed to Christ's cross.
He stripped all the spiritual tyrants in the universe of
their sham authority at the Cross and marched them
naked through the streets."

Col 2:12-15 (MSG)

When I first started my journey with Jesus, I had no grid for grace
and forgiveness. I was constantly tormented by the lies of the enemy
in my head (Rev 12:10). It was very hard for me to not only understand
what forgiveness meant, but also difficult for me to forgive myself,
and receive it as a gift from the Lord. Because my past was filled with
sex, drugs, and wild living, I was constantly blaming myself for the bad
things that I had done. I was filled with shame until I held God's Word
in my heart and declared it over my life.

Today, you may be struggling with receiving the forgiveness of God
in different areas of your life, but know that when we confess our sins
to God, He is faithful to forgive us when we mess up. He does not hold
our sins against us. This is the good news of what Jesus Christ did for us
on the cross! (1 John 1:9)

Declare God's Word over yourself, and agree with God today that
you are forgiven!

JESUS ALWAYS GOES AHEAD OF US
Chantel Garza

> "He is the rock, His works are perfect, and all His
> ways are just. A faithful God who does no wrong, upright
> and just is he."
>
> Deuteronomy 32:4 (NIV)

88

Have you ever planned something in your life like an event or a special day? Then once planned only to realize it won't be the way you expected it to be. Life can do that to us and because of this, I have learned to constantly surrender my life to Jesus and desire His plans for me. Being in His will and plans for you is the best place to be. His plans are so much better than ours.

This happened to me! The special event was my wedding that was scheduled for Nov 2020 in South Africa where I'm from, but because of Covid-19 my fiancé Ismael and I were facing too many risks that might not lead us both to the wedding. These risks lead us to have a conversation with our parents and they released us to get married in Bali. Not only did the location change but also the date. We were now scheduled to get married at the end of June, a whole five months earlier. This was very good news for us and we were so excited. It was a sad thought to think none of our families and friends from either Mexico, where he is from, or South Africa was going to be there. We still felt Jesus protecting our hearts from feeling overwhelmed.

When we stay in the place of surrender we are protected. We had so many details to consider especially because we had under a month to plan a wedding and how do you make a wedding happen during Covid-19?. The only thing I knew to do was to surrender to Jesus all the details of the wedding, the finances for everything, and our new home we had to find. The crazy thing was that before we had any conversation with our parents about the situation, a friend of mine phoned me and asked us what our wedding plans were and suggested that we should just get married at her house in Bali. At the time that didn't make sense to me but Jesus knew we were later going to be in this position and totally went ahead of us and prepared a venue for our wedding!

I remember during this time Ismael was a little worried about fi-

WINGS INTERNATIONAL

nances concerning the wedding. I just reminded him to trust in Jesus because I just knew it was going to be okay. When you go through times in your life and people around you worry and try to take things into their own hands, stop and choose to encourage them to first pray, surrender and trust in Jesus and watch what He does. Jesus was so amazing He provided for our whole wedding. I didn't have a budget for flowers and then a friend called and said she felt to pay for the flowers. We needed to get Ismael a ring, that too was provided for free and by a friend who happened to have a spare ring he didn't wear and it happened to fit him. Friends paid for parts of our honeymoon. We were going to have people bring their own food but Jesus had another idea, He put it on a friend's heart to donate money which was more than enough for the food.... WOW!!! Our friends in Bali came around us in amazing ways to bless us in so many ways!!!

Jesus is always going ahead of us. He is such a personal God. He sees you and holds your desires closely to His heart. He is our rock and when we stand surrendered we are protected and in peace knowing He has us. I pray you too will have people around you in seasons of change, don't be afraid to reach out to them in times of change for prayer or encouragement.

Today as you think of your desires, prophecies and plans, see yourself standing on a rock (which is Jesus' reliability, His love, His wisdom-raising your hands to Him in surrender and worship. Giving all that you are carrying today to Him, knowing that He sees and cares about all of it. You can fully trust Him and His goodness and timing.

TRANSCENDING THE NATURAL
Becca Giles

> "Then these righteous ones will reply, 'Lord, when
> did we ever see you hungry and feed you? Or thirsty and
> give you something to drink? Or a stranger and show
> you hospitality? Or naked and give you clothing? When
> did we ever see you sick or in prison and visit you?' And
> the King will say, 'I tell you the truth, when you did it
> to one of the least of these my brothers and sisters, you
> were doing it to me!'"
>
> Matthew 25:37-40 (NLT)

Once in Nepal, many people crowded all together in the slum area to watch and listen to the Gospel dramas. I was sitting in the dirt with the people in the crowd when a totally inebriated woman stumbled into the middle of the drama. She was a big distraction, interrupting it with loud, incoherent remarks. Suddenly, with the greatest desire I'd ever had to sit with someone in my whole life, I got up to gently take her arm and have her sit with me. She smelled so strongly of alcohol. As the drama continued to the finish, I could only sit with her, rub her back, and pray in the Spirit. I sensed that she was being abused, and began to pray deliverance and healing to her from her abuser.

Just then, a small boy from the slum came over to me and began to speak in perfect English. This boy, I believe, was an angel. He asked if he could help, and began to translate every word I said to the woman. She pulled back her hair and her sleeves to expose deep purple bruises on her forehead and her arms that were left by her husband. The little boy helped me share the Gospel and the healing that Jesus offers. She had tears running down her face as she prayed to accept Jesus into her life. Even while this happened, some men from the slum jeered and spat at us from behind.

As I only held her and scratched her back, a transcendent, supernatural exchange happened. This was Matthew 25:37-40. I was holding Jesus in my arms. I felt Jesus' back under my fingers. You and I minister directly to Jesus when we love—when we see—someone overlooked and ignored. These are not only those who have endured abuse or those who are living in a slum. They are all around, and they are in need of an encounter with Love Himself.

Caring about the attention of the "most important" doesn't lead to much; caring for the least will lead you into transforming encounters with Jesus himself as you care for the needs of His beloved. Is there anyone hurting who may need comfort today? Anyone in need? Let's go to them without thinking too much about it, and live what His Word calls us to.

91

THAT'S A REALLY BIG MOUNTAIN
Becky Blanchard

> "Jesus told them. 'I tell you the truth, if you have
> faith even as small as a mustard seed, you could say to
> this mountain, 'Move from here to there,' and it would
> move. Nothing would be impossible.'"
>
> Matthew 17:20 (ESV)

You know, there's a difference between knowing that God can do something from believing that He will do it in the circumstance that you face. Some years back, we were facing an issue at our boys' home that we helped to start in India. We had over 45 boys at a family-style home; many of them had come from living off the streets, some were orphans, and others (who had no mother) had fathers that were drug lords or in the mafia. During this time, the landlord (a devout Hindu) that we were renting from did not like the boys or the fact that they were Christian. He would treat them badly and began threatening to kick them out. We began to pray that we could own our own building. That way, we could do whatever we wanted with it.

So we prayed that God would give us a building that could serve as a home for the boys, but could also be a multipurpose center for training sessions for ministry leaders, an office, and a place to start a preschool and feeding center for the children that were living in the city trash dumps. After a long search, a two-story building was miraculously offered to us to buy. Even though the owner was Hindu and he knew it was going towards a Christian man, he offered to sell it for US$115,000. As Wings was the sole sponsor for this boys' home, we were committed to helping find a way.

That amount may seem like pennies for many businessmen and for those who have been in ministry for a long time, but it was a massive amount to me. It was a big mountain, and the owner who was offering the house gave us a deadline to pay if we wanted it. So I sent word to all of our supporters, families, friends, and anybody that I could think of, asking if they would all pray about joining in with us for this needed miracle. This amount of money was so much bigger than me and the boys' home director. I didn't know how it was going to happen. I've seen

God do miracles in my life and have seen His faithfulness and provision, but never at this amount.

I remember telling God, "Lord, this ministry is not mine. It's yours, and these children are yours, and I believe you are a good Father. If you don't do something, I don't know what we're going to do to help them. So I ask that you would move on their behalf, and I'm going to believe that you will because you are a good Father." By faith, I told the director, "Let's plan that we will own a home this year." A couple of months passed and I only received $5,000 total toward the fundraiser. But God in His faithfulness—about a month later I received a phone call from a long-time pastor friend who asked me if we still needed the money to buy the home and how serious we were about buying it. "Of course, we're serious!" I responded. "Get ready for this," the pastor said. He went on to tell me that they had just received a miraculous offering to their church and that God spoke to his heart to give part of the offering to us for this home. The offering given for us was the entire amount of $115,000!!! I was blown away and filled with joy as I told the good news to our home director there. Another mini-miracle happened after this when we were trying to make the international bank transfer to India. Things had been getting held up at that point and banks were shutting down. By a miracle, our transfer got through! And funny enough, even though it was after closing hours for the bank when the money had arrived at nighttime, our director received a phone call from them saying that it had arrived! Who calls from the bank after closing hours? It all came in just before the deadline to pay for the building! We bought it and had a big celebration and dedication party in honor of this miraculous blessing from God.

The Lord takes care of His children! Don't let a mountain in front of you become bigger to you than how great your God actually is. YOU can move mountains with your God. Only believe, even if your belief is as small as a seed, that's all you need!

WHEN JESUS SAYS 'YES,' NOBODY CAN SAY 'NO'

Fero Permatasari

"Therefore I tell you, do not worry about your life, what you will eat or drink, or about your body, what you will wear. Is not life more than food, and the body more than clothes."

Matthew 6:25 (NIV)

What do you worry about in your life? We have all worried about something, or sometimes everything. Think back to your past. Is there a time that it seemed like God missed protecting you? Look at yourself now. You are still here reading this, and everything is fine. You are still breathing, have a place to stay, have something to eat, and clothes to wear.

When I decided to live away from my family, it was tough and also a challenge for me. None of my family gave their blessing to me, and many were disappointed. But I knew this was what God wanted me to do. When He said 'yes' to me and began guiding me in His way, I learned that nobody can stop His plans, including me. I just couldn't say 'no' to what God had prepared for me because of what others wanted, or my own desires. I had to trust in His dreams for me.

What are you questioning or wondering about your future? Are you wanting to know what God has prepared for you? He knew you before you were even born, and you exist now because God has dreams for you. Your future has been prepared because our God is a dreaming God. You were included in His plan as He created this earth and everything in it. He has prepared everything for you.

He says 'yes' for you and to you. When Jesus says 'yes,' nobody can say 'no.' He says 'yes' to your tomorrow, next month, next year, your spouse, your children, your school and your job. You will be overwhelmed at everything that comes ahead when you say yes to Jesus. You and Him are one, say 'yes' to each other.

Let's pray. Father in Heaven, thank you for preparing everything that I need. Thank you for preparing my future. Help me to say 'yes' to you, and help me to trust your 'YES' for me. Amen.

CONFLICT OR CONFIDENCE BUILDERS?

Rodney Richard

"In fact, we expected to die. But as a result, we stopped relying on ourselves and learned to rely only on God, who raises the dead."

2 Corinthians 1:9 (NLT)

Over the years, when I've been faced with overwhelming circumstances, my emotions were almost too much to bear. The fear of not making it out of a situation is a paralyzing thought. When I was younger, it was a police officer pulling me over, or a girlfriend breaking up with me. As I grew older, the situations would get more serious. Every situation that I have made it through has done two things: built my confidence in God, and made me useful to others who would one day be growing through a painful experience. God is bigger. Bigger than what I've been through and bigger than what I'll ever go through.

Prayer for today: God help me not to be overwhelmed with the size of my problems today. Help me to understand that my current situation is in Your hands and that one day I'll be able to speak of Your faithfulness into someone else's life.

PROVISION
Taryon Crawford

> "And he said to His disciples, "Therefore I tell you,
> do not be anxious about your life, what you will eat, nor
> about your body, what you will put on. For life is more
> than food, and the body more than clothing. Consider
> the ravens: they neither sow nor reap, they have neither
> storehouse nor barn, and yet God feeds them. Of how
> much more value are you than the birds!"
>
> Luke 12:21-24 (ESV)

When I was 26 years old, God sent me to Scotland to serve with Youth With A Mission for about three years. This was my first time living abroad and in a communal type atmosphere. I grew up in Alabama to a single mom with four girls. We all lived in a low-income apartment. Because of my background, I was always fearful that I would not have enough money to live. However, God's ways are different than our ways and the systems of this world. The first time I experienced His financial provision in a powerful way was when I got an anonymous check from someone in our community for USD $5,500!

God had touched that person's heart, and also built my faith in Him as a good Father by letting me know that He will always provide for me and take care of me. Since then, I have had many stories of God's financial provision in my life. His promise of provision is for you too!

COUNTERFEIT LIFE
Ben Lawalata

"If you cling to your life, you will lose it; but if you
give up your life for me, you will find it."
Matthew 10:39 (NLT)

I was on my way home from work in Jakarta, driving through a toll
gate. Back then, the transactions were all in cash. As I drove away from
the booth I noticed that the bill I got back for change was counterfeit.
I didn't need a special scanner to tell that it was a counterfeit bill, it
was just that obvious. Everything about it looked and felt off. It felt like
I just lost the amount of the bill. I was too far to go back, so I kept on
going knowing that there was still one more toll fee ahead. I thought
I would pay the fee with the bill I just received. I would give away the
thing that has no value and in return, recover some portion of the value
I just lost.

As I was thinking about it, God said to me, "Or... It can all stop here
with you." I can rip the fake bill and stop it being passed around right
there with me. This means that I'd pay the price so that no one else
would have to anymore. I knew what God was trying to teach me. Firstly,
yes, Jesus did that! He paid the price, so we get to have life. The curse of
sin ended with Him when He died on the cross so you and I can have life
through His death. Secondly, Jesus is the only one who can do it because
only in Him is the truth and the life.

Without Jesus, we would try to figure out our ways of life as if everyone was writing some value on a blank bill. If you own a business
empire, you're worth more. If you're famous, the bigger your value is.
Yet still, none of it would be real because no one would really know true
life. We would just be passing around counterfeits. We would trade with
each other and be consumed by this void pursuit of higher value. We
would even flag our fake bills at God and say, "I know life. Here it is. I
don't need you."

If this was all we knew about life, yes it would be hard to let it go.
It would only feel like giving up life. But with Jesus, the price has been
paid. What we do now is to open up our fists, give it up, and receive
what Jesus offers in return; real life. We're not just receiving a portion

of our value, but whole-fully and abundantly. We get to live in freedom. Our life doesn't have to be about pursuing life, it's here, with Jesus. Our value is secured.

JESUS IS YOUR NUMBER ONE CHEERLEADER!
Chantel Garza

"Now it is God who makes both us and you stand
firm in Christ. He has anointed us, set a seal of ownership on us, and put His Spirit in our hearts as a deposit,
guaranteeing what is to come."

2 Corinthians 1:21-22 (NIV)

Jesus is so many things for us. He is our healer, provider, savior, and friend. He also came to show us what God the Father is like. My life has been a process of understanding what it means to be called a child of God, and to see God as my Father. Some of you may not have had a father that was a great role model for you. Maybe he wasn't present, or you never met Him, or you have experienced abuse. All these factors can influence our relationship with Jesus—how we see Him and how we see ourselves. When I read this scripture it encouraged me so much!

Here it is in The Passion Translation:

"Now it is God Himself who has anointed us. And He is constantly strengthening both His seal of love over our hearts and has given us the Holy Spirit like an engagement ring is given to a bride- a down payment of the blessings to come!" [emphasis added]

Wow, this spoke to me of a father that pursues us. God encourages us to stand firm, reminds us of the truth, and even at times rebukes us because He has better plans for us.This is all done with unconditional love. We have a God who is personally cheering us on to make sure we stand firm till the end. We have a Father that doesn't give up on us. He wants us to rely on Him. He has set a seal of ownership on us. We have a father and a friend that wants a relationship with us— a father that sees us and loves us. Maybe you haven't known what it feels like to be loved without conditions. No matter what you have done or gone through, Jesus loves you the same today, yesterday, and will love you tomorrow. I want to encourage you to receive His love for yourself today.

I will never forget when Jesus spoke to me in the village in Bali while I was having an insecure moment. I was struggling to see who I am in His eyes and didn't know if I could do what He had asked me to do for the people in the village. He showed me a picture where I was sitting with Him, fully in His embrace. He encouraged me saying, "If you only knew, my daughter, your place in my arms, you would know you can do all things."

As we live in His truth for us, of who we are in His word, and who He says He is for us, we are changed. We are then able to love without barriers even if we are not loved back. We can honor others above ourselves, live in joy, and live in confidence knowing that we are forever found in His arms. We can do anything because He is with us; He is not far away.

100

Prayer: Jesus, I am so thankful for you today. Thank you for always pursuing me!

Holy Spirit, please remind me of the Father's heart for me. Thank you, Jesus, for anointing me, for constantly helping and encouraging me in how to stand firm. Remind me of your truth when life gets hard, and when I feel insecure. I am so thankful for your love for me today! Amen.

THE BLIND WOMAN SAW AGAIN
David Blanchard

"Jesus answered, 'It was neither that this man
sinned, nor his parents; but it was in order that the
works of God might be displayed in him.'"

John 9:3 (NASB)

One time early on in our Mexico ministry, we went up to a ranch
village south of Matehuala called "San Juan Sin Agua," which means
"Saint John Without Water." It hardly ever rained in this arid, desert
ranch village. We had a crusade in one of the churches with Pastor Si-
mon Reyes. There was standing room only. The rectangle church had
block walls and a metal roof with a dirt floor. There were many people
who gave their hearts to the Lord. We asked if anyone needed the Lord
to touch them for restoration from a physical sickness or problem. After we had prayed for several people, I asked an older lady what she
needed. She said that her left eye had a cataract and that she was blind
in that eye. She wanted God to heal her. There were no windows in the
church anymore because the rowdy neighbors and unbelievers threw
rocks through them, and later they were closed up with concrete blocks.
As I was praying for the woman, all of a sudden she let out a loud cry
that echoed off of the tin roof. She started to shout, "I can see, I can
see, I can see!" Everyone was shocked. As I looked at the lady, she kept
explaining that now she could see. It excited her so much, and I was
startled as I had just seen God restore the sight of someone for the first
time. Praise the Lord!

To understand this miracle better, I must explain something. When
the woman told me that she was blind in her left eye and she wanted
to see again, I thought, "Oh Lord, I don't have the ability to do that. I
don't have the faith that it takes to return sight to someone." Somebody
once said that there has been a lot of empty hands laid on empty heads.
Meaning that many times when we pray, we don't have the faith to believe for the healing or miracle, and the person that we lay our hands on
doesn't have the faith either to believe for the restoration. So it is very
important to remember that our faith must be in Jesus Christ because
He said that all things are possible to him who believes. In the verse that

we just read in John, it talks about the blind man who was born blind in order that the works of God might be displayed in him. Jesus healed the blind man by the power of God that was working through him. We can pray for people, help people, and see people healed by the power of God that is working in us as we put our trust and faith in God who is the Savior, the healer, and the miracle worker.

Isaiah 30:3-6 says that we are to encourage the sick and the tired; strengthen the weak and feeble, and say to those with an anxious heart, "Take courage, fear not." It says, "Behold your God will come with recompense and he will save you. Then the eyes of the blind will be opened and the ears of the deaf will be unstopped and the lame will leap like a deer and the tongue of the dumb will shout for joy. For the waters will break forth in the wilderness!" We must trust in the Lord with all of our heart, with all of our soul, and with all of our might because all things are possible with God! After the blind woman was healed and received her sight, the people began to shout with joy and we praised the Lord for a long time. That night God made history in a little ranch town that had very little water ever running through it. God Almighty poured out his living water upon this little village and revival broke out in that church as the people were eyewitnesses of the living God!

John 9:4 says that we must work the works of God who sent Jesus, as long as it is day, for the night is coming when no man can work. We must be about God the Father's business like never before. His heartbeat is that none would perish and that all would be saved. That must be our heartbeat also! Put your trust in God. Believe God. Believe God's Word. Believe the promises in God's Word. Allow the Holy Spirit of God to use you to touch the lives of those around you because it's time to make history for the kingdom of God! God is in you desiring to do His works through you. You have his light and anointing shining through you in this dark and needy world. Let God work through you. Let God show the world his love, power, and salvation through you!

SEASONS
Ricardo Rayon

"For our present troubles are small and won't last very long. Yet they produce for us a glory that vastly outweighs them and will last forever."
2 Corinthians 4:17 (NLT)

"For everything there is a season, a time for every activity under heaven."
Ecclesiastes 3:1 (NLT)

"Yet God has made everything beautiful for its own time. He has planted eternity in the human heart."
Ecclesiastes 3:11 (NLT)

I lived a short season in Wisconsin, USA. It was the first time I experienced the extremes of the four seasons. From a hot and humid summer where everything is green, a fall that is a little bit chilly and all the trees turn red and orange, a very cold winter where it snowed for days, to a warm and welcoming spring. I learned there is a season for everything. Life is not always awesome, but it's not always horrible either. Whatever you are experiencing now, good or bad, shall pass. The only thing that stays the same is Jesus, His word, and His presence.

When I first moved to Asia, I lived for six months in Nepal. Everything was new, and it was incredible. I was in love with the place, the people, and everything was wonderful. I was convinced that it was the place that God had for me. I didn't want that time to end. The next year I returned for six months in Nepal, and everything was the complete opposite. Everything went wrong and I ended up exhausted from ministry, people, and life in general. That year was very difficult in many aspects; my personal life, ministerial, economic, family, etc, and I thought that time would never end. After all that happened, the season ended, and it ended well.

Good seasons and bad seasons don't last forever. Everything shall pass. We have good seasons and bad seasons—that's life. But in both, God is there. In both seasons, good and bad, the Word of God is real, and

Faith Food Devotional

He is faithful! Now, wherever you are or whatever season you are in, be encouraged that God is with you, He loves you, and He will bring peace, hope, and joy. Don't be afraid. Jesus is with you, and God sends His Holy Spirit to be with you and lead you through it all.

WINGS INTERNATIONAL

UNSTOPPABLE
Becky Blanchard

"You, dear children, are from God and have overcome
them, because the one who is in you is greater than the
one who is in the world."

1 John 4:4 (NIV)

One time I was leading a church team on a trip to China. We were in
the mountains ministering there to the kids and families that lived in
the mountainside area. Most of the parents were poor farmers and had
very little to live off of. It was the month of December, so we decided to
bring the families some food gift bags and other necessary household
items as a Christmas blessing. Our plan was to split into two groups
and hike the different narrow paths on the hills to go to each of the
homes. The families were so receptive and thankful for the gesture. In
the beauty of their culture, they invited us in to sit down to have some
hot green tea together. Later with one of the teams, we left one house
and started down the hill toward another home. As we walked down
the path, we approached one building that had a massive, scary-looking
dog at the entrance of it. He was barking and growling at us with foamy
slime dripping from his mouth! Not the kind of dog you would want to
mess with! He was angry and startled us, making us all stop where we
were. I thought to myself, "Should we keep walking and try to ignore
him, or is that a dumb idea for the crew with me?" We took a couple
more steps forward and he got even angrier. At that moment when we
were frozen in our tracks, I felt the Holy Spirit remind me that He was
with us and that we were the ones with authority. We were on a mission
for God—why should we let anything stop us?! As soon as I heard this
reminder in my heart, I quickly shouted back at the dog, "Be quiet in the
name of Jesus! And you stay right there!" I kid you not, right after that
the dog yelled out a loud "Yelp!" His tale went in between his legs, and
he turned around and backed off! We were all like, "Daang, go Jesus!"
We continued on and got to visit many more families, hear their stories,
and introduce them to the Savior. Some were even so touched that they
insisted we share a meal with them of some of their most prized meat
and rice. We were so humbled by the generosity of these sweet farmers.

Faith Food Devotional

For most of us at some point, when attempting to walk in the path of God's will for our life, the enemy will try to stop it from happening. He doesn't want you to move forward or to progress in the plan God wants to bring to pass for you and through you. Don't you dare let any thing, any devil, or any lie of opposition hold you back from moving forward in God's purpose for you! The greater one lives inside you, so the enemy is the one that should retreat and be afraid, not you. Pick up your sword, God is with you!

ONE VOICE AMONGST MANY
Stephen Walter

> "God has given each of you a gift from His great vari-
> ety of spiritual gifts. Use them well to serve one another.
> Do you have the gift of speaking? Then speak as though
> God Himself were speaking through you. Do you have
> the gift of helping others? Do it with all the strength and
> energy that God supplies. Then everything you do will
> bring glory to God through Jesus Christ. All glory and
> power to him forever and ever! Amen."
>
> 1 Peter 4:10-11 (NLT)

I was never the best musician. Although I tried extremely hard in class, and at times saw great improvement, there was always someone better than me. Being a string bass player, it was hard to see my importance in the grand scheme of the orchestral sound. Don't get me wrong, I loved the pieces we played and the feeling of being a part of something greater, but the feeling of importance never really sank in. What really kept me going on the musical path was my middle/high school orchestra director. He saw the importance of music and its effect on the growing minds of the youth, and more often than not, he gave very passionate speeches of his efforts to keep music alive in our curriculum. When it came time to choose the next step in my journey to adulthood, I chose to pursue a degree in music education because of the inspiration my director instilled in me. In entering the prestigious realm of music within the university setting, I was met with great favor. The story of passing my entrance audition in itself is a miracle, but that is a story for another time.

I remember one cold winter afternoon walking to the practice hall for rehearsal. Upon arrival, I made my way to my usual spot to unpack and tune. We took the stage to begin rehearsal, spot-checking individual sections to blend the right tone, and singling out problem spots to be focused on in individual practice times. Everything seemed like another rehearsal, but as we began to run the piece in its entirety, I felt something unusual. During a part where the bass section was at rest, I looked over the orchestra, gazing at each individual member and noticing the subtle differences of everyone. Each person had a uniqueness about them; whether it was the way they dressed, their playing position, the way they moved, or even how they tapped their foot to keep time. At that moment, it wasn't just an orchestra, but a collection of unique individuals all working towards a common goal of creating something beautiful and special. In that moment, God told me something I will never forget. He said that this sound we were creating was one of a kind because of everyone that was helping to create it. Everyone, from the first chairs to the last, and the quietest to the loudest, gave this music a heavenly characteristic that could never be duplicated by another group. He said that my sound added something to the music that could never be recreated. I was overwhelmed with love and joy. It was like I was hearing the music for the first time, and this time, I could hear everyone's spirit being poured out in unison with love, joy, dedication, and diligence. I could feel God's presence standing with me saying, "Your sound matters. Your voice matters. This music wouldn't be as beautiful without you."

God not only opened my eyes to see my importance within the orchestra but also in life.

We all have a unique sound, a unique voice, that no one else on this planet has. God's word says that you are fearfully and wonderfully made and that He has chosen YOU to live at this time and to be the person He created you to be. This world would not be as beautiful if it didn't have you. Peoples' lives would be different if you weren't here to impact them in your own unique way. However small you think your actions may be, however quiet you think your voice is, it matters. It matters to God, and to the beauty and music that is life on this earth. The magnificent orchestra of God's creation depends on you realizing that, although you are one voice amongst many, one sound amongst an orchestra, it would not be as beautiful if it didn't have you.

TO BE MORE LIKE JESUS
Fero Permatasari

"Just as the Son of Man did not come to be served,
but to serve, and to give His life as a ransom for many."
Matthew 20:28 (NIV)

"Blessed is the one who perseveres under trial
because, having stood the test, that person will receive
the crown of life that the Lord has promised to those
who love Him."
James 1:12 (NIV)

There was a man who came to this earth and He did a lot of things: He healed people, He shared stories, He taught people, He fed people, He did miracles, and He also died on a cross. He said, "Father, forgive them, for they do not know what they are doing."

It was Jesus; He died for you and me. He did that because He loves us, He is that love. It is more than enough for me to know that, in this broken world, somebody died for me. Knowing that I am loved by someone in this way blows my mind. The world rejected Him, but He still gave His life for us. He is full of unconditional love. Because of that love, we can be saved, we can be forgiven, and we can have hope.

In my life, I was greatly impacted by someone I once knew as I witnessed how he surrendered his all, his life, and everything he had to serve Jesus. His desire was to be more like Jesus, and this really encouraged me to do the same in how I lived my life. Even though it's not always easy, Jesus is always with us every step of the way.

You may be in a season where you feel rejected, or feel judged by the community surrounding you. You may feel dry from continually serving people, pouring your all out, and wondering why it is hard to follow Jesus. Let me tell you that you are actually showing God's love to people and God sees you. You are doing what He did. In Luke 9:23 Jesus said, "Whoever wants to be my disciple must deny themselves and take up their cross daily and follow me." Being more like Jesus is far from being comfortable, and you may not always have the world's approval. However, you were born with purpose; one purpose, and a different calling

Faith Food Devotional

than anyone else. Stay faithful in serving where you are and trust Him as you will have the reward that God has prepared for you.

Let's pray: Father in Heaven, help me to keep my focus on you. Sometimes, I don't know what to do, where to go, or what to say. But as long as I know you are leading me, I will trust you. Help me to remember what Jesus went through so that, even when things are not easy, I know you will always be there for me. Amen.

JOY CAN REMAIN!
Chantel Garza

"Let the morning bring me word of your unfailing
love, for I have put my trust in you. Show me the way I
should go, for I entrust my life. Teach me to do your will,
for you are my God, may your good spirit lead me on
level ground."

Psalm 143:8,10 (NIV)

We all live through seasons in our lives. Some seasons will be a time where we need to sow seed and work at the ground (which is hard work and requires faithfulness). There will be seasons where you will see life, growth, change, or restfulness. Then, there will be a season where there is much fruit and excitement. Only Jesus knows how long we will be in each season in our lives. Our job is to seek Him for what He is teaching us in each season, stay close to Him, remember His words, and seek Him on how we can remain in the race with Him.

In my third year being a part of Wings International, three of us on the team went for three nights each week to our center in the village. The people living there were Hindu. We would share Jesus with them through teaching English, sports, dance, through Gospel movies in their language, or through our own personal testimonies while we formed deeper relationships together. Jesus gave us favor with the community living there and we were so thankful for that. Throughout that year, I remember feeling that my joy at times wasn't there. I became discouraged, but I knew I couldn't give up because of Jesus' love for these people.

As the year was ending, I sought Jesus for the next year ahead, knowing that I needed to go through this year for a reason, but also not wanting to run the same way I had been going into the new year. I felt the Lord revealed two very important things.

Firstly, I need to carry the weapons of praise and faith. I need to praise Him and magnify Him over what I see. This will increase my faith, and my JOY will remain... and it did!

Secondly, He told me that my joy would come from me constantly remembering that HE was in control and that I wasn't. When I planned my teaching lessons, I felt in control because I knew what was expected from me and therefore I found joy. But as for the rest, I didn't know what I was doing when it came to the relationship-building or bringing a village into the knowledge of Jesus—especially in another language. Having feelings like that is okay, but it shouldn't steal my joy. His voice that day eliminated any striving in me, it changed my perspective and removed any pressure I had to make something happen in my own understanding. The lie was broken that what I had to give wasn't enough, and it brought such freedom. MY JOY REMAINED! It is possible to have our joy remain in whatever season we find ourselves in.

(We'll use Psalm 143 as a prayer because the Word turned into prayer is so powerful!) Prayer: Jesus, thank you for today! I ask that each morning as I seek you I would hear your word of unfailing love. I put my trust in you again today. Please show me the way that I should go. I entrust my day and life to you. Please teach me to do your will today, for you are my God and I love you. Holy Spirit, please lead me on level ground all the days of my life. Amen.

MY TEMPLE, YOUR TEMPLE
Becky Blanchard

> "Don't you realize that your body is the temple of
> the Holy Spirit, who lives in you and was given to you by
> God? You do not belong to yourself."
> 1 Corinthians 6:19 (NLT)

> "But you will receive power when the Holy Spirit comes upon you.
> And you will be my witnesses, telling people about me everywhere—in
> Jerusalem, throughout Judea, in Samaria, and to the ends of the earth."
> Acts 1:8 (NLT)

The word "temple" is a term more relatable to eastern culture. To western culture, buildings used for religious meetings are just normally known as churches in relation to Christian influence. But in Asia and in Bali, temples are a way of life. Basically, a temple is a building dedicated to spiritual practices, whether praying to or chanting to or singing to other gods or idols or spirits. One time I was on a motorbike heading home after our kids' outreach had finished. It was around the time of the year where there were a lot of Hindu ceremonies going on. As I was passing this one Hindu temple, I could hear loud chanting, clanging of cymbals, and other racket growing louder and louder. Honestly, the atmosphere that I was driving by started to disturb me inside. I had my headphones on, and I quickly turned up the song I was listening to, "Tremble" by Mosaic. I was getting ready to sing the lyrics, "Jesus, Jesus. You make the darkness tremble.." as loud as I could. And just as I was about to sing, I heard the Holy Spirit stop me and say, "Becky, you don't even have to shout or be loud. You can just whisper the name of Jesus and it's more powerful than all that clamor and their yelling and noise." The feeling of that revelation was so cool! I could literally feel His light illuminate in my heart in the middle of that darkness. So I whispered the song as passionately as I could the rest of the way home.

James 2:19 says that demons tremble at our God! His name is above all names! We have this joke with our team that we'll just go with sledgehammers to all the temples and altars and knock them down for Jesus. That's how we'll bring them to Christ. NOT!!! That's not the way to destroy the presence of evil or to build God's kingdom. The power is in the Gospel, aka GOOD NEWS. The power is in His Spirit and presence living within us. We are His carriers, His temples.

That's why sometimes, when I'm walking around my neighborhood passing temples and I see some of the Hindus offering incense and saying prayers, I just start speaking or singing the word of God into the atmosphere, over that neighborhood, and over the homes as I'm passing. Just those very simple actions, because of who I am and who I carry within me, are powerful. As I write this, I've recently just moved into a new place and I happen to live near a massive Hindu temple. Driving by it one day, the thought occurred to me, "My temple is more powerful than that one." It's true, because of Who is inside me!

Maybe you're not in a country where there is a Hindu temple on every street corner, but the spirit world is the real deal. It just looks different depending on where you're at.

The enemy just looks for access points, places of permission, and an open door for him to come and make himself at home and set up shop... aka a stronghold. His goal is to take territory.

Take it back.

Take back whatever territory you've given to the enemy or that the enemy has taken from you. Even your presence in your community is a game-changer! The greatest presence in the universe lives within you. Speak the word of God out loud over the area, over the people where you're at. You don't have to be all weird and do that in front of them, twirling or drawing attention to yourself. Even if they're right in front of you, you can do it under your breath. You don't have to be loud, I mean you can if you want, but the cool thing is it's not even necessary! Do you know what you have? The presence of who you have within you is potent! May your 'temple' be a channel that God can use to bring transformation to wherever you're at.

Pray: Jesus, help me to have your power. Please fill me with your Holy Spirit and boldness to be the kind of person that affects the atmosphere wherever I go because of your presence that I carry within.

CHOOSE TO FOLLOW JESUS
Ria Lowing

"But whatever were gains to me I now consider loss
for the sake of Christ. What is more, I consider everything a loss because of the surpassing worth of knowing Christ Jesus my Lord, for whose sake I have lost all
things. I consider them garbage, that I may gain Christ
and be found in Him, not having a righteousness of my
own that comes from the law, but that which is through
faith in Christ—the righteousness that comes from God
on the basis of faith."

115

Philippians 3:7-9 (NIV)

"As they were walking along the road, a man said to
Him, 'I will follow you wherever you go.' Jesus replied,
'Foxes have dens and birds have nests, but the Son of
Man has no place to lay His head.' He said to another
man, 'Follow me'. But he replied, 'Lord, first let me go
and bury my father.' Jesus said to him, 'Let the dead bury
their own dead, but you go and proclaim the kingdom
of God.' Still another said, 'I will follow you, Lord; but
first let me go back and say goodbye to my family.' Jesus
replied, 'No one who puts a hand to the plow and looks
back is fit for service in the kingdom of God.'"

Luke 9:57-62 (NIV)

In 2015, I reached what I was dreaming for in my career. I was trusted to be the director of a branch contractor company. I was also a leader
in my connect group at church at that time, and everything was going
perfectly. My career was going well, and my personal relationship with
God was intimate. During one of my devotional times at the end of the
year, the Lord spoke to me through those Bible verses in Luke 9.

God wanted me to be His disciple and share the Gospel. I was called
to submit myself and my time to follow Jesus. He called me to give everything I had, my career as a director, my connect group friends, and
even my family.

Faith Food Devotional

"And everyone who has left houses or brothers or sisters or father or mother or children or fields for my sake will receive a hundred times as much and will inherit eternal life." Matthew 19:29

I decided to give everything to be His disciple. It is not an easy thing for us to do when we've got everything on this earth, like wealth, or a career, or family. It's hard for us to let them go to follow Jesus. I left my passion as a director in that contractor company and joined a mission group to go to neglected tribes. I left my hometown, friends, and family to go to an uncomfortable place. I'll still continue to be faithful because I want to be His disciple.

When I left the things that matter in the world's eyes to make Jesus number one in my life, so many things that I never could've imagined happened. Even until now, I have been cared for by God. When I decided to follow Jesus completely, I began to see people delivered, people getting healed, people coming back to the Father, and getting baptized. When I witnessed all these miracles happening through my life, I felt it was better than winning the lottery.

The best choice you can ever make in life is to follow Jesus with everything. You can place your future in His hands, and see Him meet with you in whatever you ask.

THROUGH THE UNCOMFORTABLE
Becca Giles

> "And we know that God causes all things to work
> together for good to those who love God, to those who
> are called according to His purpose."
>
> Romans 8:28 (NASB)

I was assigned to co-lead a mission trip to Mexico for a group of school of ministry students. This was my first experience being designated a leadership role for a group of people this big and a trip like this—I felt rather important. We arrived at the airport, excited for what Jesus was going to do. I went up to check-in at the counter, and the woman behind the desk said to me, "Maam, I'm sorry to tell you this, but your passport is expired. You cannot leave the country until you get it renewed."

I kept a forced, positive face on and told the team that I would sort out getting a new passport to meet them in Mexico shortly. We said our goodbyes and everyone went around a corner to go through airport security. Once they were out of sight, I was a total mess. I cried on the phone with the school of ministry director, and my parents had to come to pick me up. Thoroughly embarrassed, I felt like a big, fat failure. At home, I wallowed in my disappointment for two days while I was in the process of getting an expensive, expedited passport. I really complained to God more than I ever had in my life. Finally, on the third morning, I asked the Lord what He could speak to me through this.

"Read Romans 5," He said to me gently. Romans 5:3-5 says, "We can rejoice, too, when we run into problems and trials, for we know that they help us develop endurance. And endurance develops strength of character, and character strengthens our confident hope of salvation. And this hope will not lead to disappointment. For we know how dearly God loves us, because He has given us the Holy Spirit to fill our hearts with His love."

Somehow humbled and encouraged at the same time, I repented for complaining and began to see my setback through different eyes. I want to make this clear first: God wasn't sitting on his throne in heaven, laughing at me when I was crying in the airport. Good fathers don't set

Faith Food Devotional

up unfortunate events to happen to their children to teach them a lesson. Our Good Father can, however, use anything that we walk through to lead us into revelation, to tenderly teach us if we need, or to grow us. And it won't lead to disappointment.

When those experiences come and try to shake you, I pray that your hope in Jesus would intensify within you, and lead you to take God at His word; He causes all things (which includes the awkward and embarrassing) to work together for the good for those who love Him and are called to His purposes.

God quickly joined me back to the team in Mexico, and we saw hundreds of people healed and saved on that trip. My faith matured, my character was strengthened, and that trace of pride that was hidden in me was humbled.

Through the uncomfortable, keep leaning into the Father. He is truly for you in every way, and He is more than enough for you to draw from as you trust in Him.

YOUR FRIDGE WILL NEVER BE EMPTY
Steve Lunn

"Seek the Kingdom of God above all else, and live
righteously, and He will give you everything you need."
Matthew 6:33 (NLT)

Four years ago, when we arrived here in Indonesia to serve the Lord,
my wife opened up the refrigerator—and God spoke to her! He said,
"Kim, your refrigerator will never be empty!" That's an amazing promise
because it meant that God would take responsibility for feeding us! We
had three hungry kids, so it's a pretty big responsibility, right?

So—of course—our three children grow up in our home, understanding that when our family follows God in faith, we can expect to see
miracles! Just the other day, our 10-year old daughter, Genesis, walks
over to the refrigerator and flings the door open to see what she can find
to eat. Seeing that there was very little food left inside, she announces
loudly to the whole household: "Our fridge is almost empty! It's time for
God to do something!"

Guess what? Two hours later there was a knock on our door. When
we opened the door, it was one of our friends who owned a restaurant
down the road. She and her family had been praying and decided they
should bring us some vegetables, but they brought us TOO MANY! We
couldn't possibly fit them all inside our fridge! My wife and I pastor a
church, so I quickly grabbed my phone to see who else in our church
did not have enough food to eat. Then we got some bags, filled them
with the extra vegetables, and delivered them to fifteen other people!
God didn't just feed our family of five people; He fed a total of twenty
people! The amazing thing is that one of the grandmas that got the food
was so happy because she had just run out of food. She was literally
praying to God for food for her family when I called.

Isn't God amazing? Not only did He keep his promise that our fridge
would never be empty, but He also gave us such tremendous joy because
we got to share with others as well! It's very important that you understand this: always look for ways to bless other people! Don't try to keep
things for yourself. God gives us EVERYTHING (including his own Son!)
so we are so full of joy to share what we have with others!

Faith Food Devotional

A HEARING HEART
Donna Blanchard

"My sheep listen to My voice; I know them, and they
follow Me."

John 10:27 (NIV)

I have been in the ministry full-time for almost 40 years now. In 1986, my husband and I and our two girls left Kansas to become missionaries in Mexico. Throughout the years, many people would ask me how I knew I was called to full-time ministry. They would ask me, "When did you feel the call to be a missionary to Mexico?" I told them, "To be honest, I have never received a call to go specifically to Mexico, or anywhere else for that matter." You see, when you love the Lord, your heart's desire is to hear his voice and obey. I remember when I was 19 years old, I was praying about where I would go to finish my university studies. I had been attending a two-year college in my hometown and I was looking for a university to finish my college education.

I was raised in a small town, Garden City, Kansas, with a total population of 35,000 people. Living in that small town, I was not aware of how many universities there were in the state of Kansas. I knew that I would have to continue to pay for my own college education and I could not afford to go outside my state. At that time, I knew of only three universities, and I had reasons why I did not want to go to any of those. One day, as I was sitting in one of my classes, I looked over across the room and saw a young lady wearing a T-shirt; on the front of the T-shirt it stated in big bold letters, "Emporia State University." Immediately after I read that, I heard the Holy Spirit speak to me in my heart in a still small voice (kind of like a strong thought); He said, "That's where you're going to go to school next year." After class, I immediately went up to the girl and asked her, "Emporia State University—is that in the state of Kansas?" She said, "Yes, it's located in the eastern part of Kansas." I looked at her and said, "Ok. That's where I'm going to school next year." She gave me a funny look as if to say, "You didn't even know where it was." I immediately left class and found more information about it, and filled out the application. I worked all summer long on a construction site and I saved every penny for college. That fall, I packed up all my earthly belongings into my car. It was not the greatest car, so I prayed hard that I would make it through the 6-hour drive! As I was pulling out of my hometown, I looked in the rearview mirror and I knew inside my heart I would never live there again. I did not know what the future held, but I did know God told me to go.

When I got settled, I found a church that was very passionate and had a Bible study for college students. I started attending the study; and that is where I just happened to meet my future husband, David Blanchard (or was that God's plan after all?). I had no idea David was living there as the director of Youth for Christ. He later told me that he was on his knees every night praying, "God, send me my wife." Now, I want to remind you, when I was sitting in my junior college class reading that young ladies T-shirt, the Holy Spirit did not tell me to 'go to Emporia State University AND you will meet your husband.' No, He simply said, "You're going there next year."

I remember David asking me when we were dating, "Do you feel called to India?" He then said, "I feel I am called to be a missionary, do you feel called to be a missionary?" I looked at him and said, "I have never heard a call from God to be a missionary, but if He calls me to marry you, wherever you're called I will be called also." (I didn't even know that was a verse in the book of Ruth.)

The key is obedience. God leads step-by-step; after we complete the first step, He shows us the next one. He wants us to obey Him even if He doesn't tell you the final outcome. The word 'obey' means: "to follow the commands or guidance of another person." Now in Hebrew; there is no word for 'obey.' Where we translate 'obey' in the bible, the Hebrew word is 'shema' which means 'a hearing heart'—that's important. A 'hearing heart' is a heart that is intent on; or committed to, doing whatever God commands: whatever He asks from us.

You see, God does not call those that look like they are so prepared, qualified, and talented. No, God decides to call you in your weakness, your unqualified state, and as you answer that call, hear and obey His voice, you will see He always calls the obedient. I would've never imagined that after 27 years in the ministry we would see the fulfillment of the vision God gave my husband and I to see one million people give their lives to Jesus Christ and to give out one million Bibles—but it happened, one step after another. It all begins with having a hearing heart to the Lord's voice and stepping out in faith.

Faith Food Devotional

WAIT ON THE LORD
Rob Giles

> "But those who wait on the Lord shall renew their
> strength; They shall mount up with wings like eagles,
> they shall run and not be weary, they shall walk and not
> faint."
>
> Isaiah 40:31 (NKJV)

Have you ever really thought about how much time you spend wait-ing for things? We wait for food when we go to a restaurant, or when we stand in lines at the grocery store, or waiting for something to arrive in the mail; the point is, there are many things in life that we find our-selves waiting for. The problem is that in today's society, we want things right away, or we are in so much of a hurry most of the time that it is frustrating to even have to wait at all.

In our lives with God, the importance that we give to the time ele-ment of our lives is crucial. Have you ever given considerable thought to how much time we spend waiting on things that are far less important than waiting on the Lord? Waiting on the Lord is the only kind of wait-ing that comes with a promise of strength for us (like it says in Isaiah 40:31). There have been times in my life when I felt like I was waiting forever for an answer for direction, peace about a situation in life, or something having to do with a job or a promotion. Whatever it was, when I put my attention on Jesus and began fully trusting and wait-ing on Him (rather than just waiting for the answer or the outcome), it always surpassed anything else that I could've done throughout that waiting.

It may not be easy to wait on the Lord, but it will be worth it. He promises strength for those in the waiting, and He is always faithful and true.

I'M GOING TO BE WITH YOU!

Ismael Garza

> "And teach them to do everything I have told you. I
> will be with you always, even until the end of the world."
> Matthew 28:20 (CEV)

God's promise is that He will never leave us alone. I want to tell you 123 a story about when Jesus made this promise real to me. It happened on one of our many trips to the village where we have a community center in Bali. At this point, we had been going to this center for two years, and our relationships and trust had been built with the people living there.

There was one boy, Agus, who I had grown very fond of, and we often spent time together while we were in the village. In Indonesia, many people believe in ghosts that are called "pocong". One day, all of our students in the community center were talking about this kind of ghost, and that it made some of them so scared, especially at nighttime.

This particular night, I was about to throw the trash away outside, but because we don't have very much light, I asked Agus to come with me. As we were walking, I asked Agus, "Are you scared of the pocong pocong?" His answer surprised me. He replied, "No, because Jesus is with me." That was a miracle moment, and I had a glimpse of how this entire generation was going to come to believe in Jesus. This village has been so closed to the Gospel and closed to any people bringing the Gospel for many years before. That night, I got to witness and be a part of hearing how this little boy believed that Jesus was with him and that he knew he didn't need to be scared.

Today I want to encourage you that just like this little boy, you too can believe that Jesus is with you and that you don't need to fear anything. Jesus is always with you and won't leave you! And, to you who have been sowing seeds into people's lives about Jesus—don't give up! One day, I believe you will see the fruit of that truth you've sown into that person made real.

LIGHT MY WAY
Becky Blanchard

> "Your word is a lamp to my feet and a light to my
> path."
>
> Psalm 119:105 (NIV)

> "Let me hear in the morning of your steadfast love,
> for in you I trust. Make me know the way I should go, for
> to you I lift up my soul."
>
> Psalm 143:8 (NIV)

Throughout the seasons of my life, the Bible, the word of God, has seriously been a flashlight from God that has guided me every step of the way. From my daily scripture reading, many times He will speak to me on an area of my life I'm needing guidance in at that moment. Sometimes, it even coincides with the Bible devotion plan I'm on. That might seem like a coincidence, but God is bigger than that and it's no coincidence. There have also been other times where I'll hear Him speak to my heart to look up a specific Bible passage to read.

I'll give you an example of some of these instances in my life. One was when I first moved to Asia to live in Hong Kong. I went to work for a ministry whose vision was also similar to what God had placed in my heart for Asia. "Perfect fit," I thought. God was so faithful throughout all my preparations to move there; I was able to sell my car and some other positions I had, and raise the funds that I'd needed to go. But when I got there, only three months after I arrived, the couple I moved to work there with had to move back to America for family emergency reasons. So there I was, on my own in Hong Kong, and not really knowing anyone very well at the time. Thankfully though, the couple had connected me to a great pastor and church there; but I was still a little bewildered as to what I was supposed to do from that point on. I just kept asking God in my morning devotion time, "God, you have to show me what to do. What am I supposed to do now?" Then, during my daily reading, I opened up to Psalm 37. Right there in verse 3 He spoke to me so clearly, "Trust in the Lord and do good; dwell in the land and cultivate faithfulness..." I knew God was telling me to stay there. He knew all this was going to happen ahead of time when He led me to come and He was going to work it out. All I was to do was to trust Him, be faithful, and do what I knew to do. I volunteered at that local church for a period of time, and soon after we got to know each other better, was offered a job as Outreach Pastor! Outreach ministry to those not yet in church was more my background and passion and I loved serving there. I'm so grateful for what God did in that season of my life.

Another story I'll share is of the time when the COVID-19 epidemic first broke out. All of the Wings foreign staff (those of us not from Indonesia) were concerned about our visas which were processing; we weren't sure whether we would be kicked out as they expired during the lock-down. Not really knowing what was going to happen or what to do, I asked God to give some direction.

In my morning time with God, I felt like He spoke to me about a certain scripture to read. I wasn't positive if it was God or me, but I heard the scripture passage repeated in my head again. So I looked it up. It was Isaiah 52:14 which says, "But you will not leave in haste or go in flight; for the Lord will go before you, the God of Israel will be your rear guard." Ok then, that was pretty clear. We knew God was telling us, "Don't worry! You won't have to panic and leave in a hurry!" The amazing thing is that God gave us favor with immigration and we didn't have to leave! Even though there had been some announcements going around that made it sound like we would have to, His word and will prevailed. Guidance from the Bible isn't always that specific, but the more we read it, we learn to better recognize God's peace, His wisdom, and His voice in our hearts for our journey.

The Bible is more than a rule book or just stories; it is alive and it is the life-force we need each step of the way to propel us into the future that God has laid out for us! He wants to speak to you each day and guide you if you give Him space for it. He cares about your day-to-day and even the matters of your life at home, your family, or your work. Give the Word of God an important place in your life and daily schedule and decisions. You can pray, "God help me to recognize your voice more clearly in my life. Help my decisions to be mapped out by your guidance. And give me more understanding as I read your word. Amen."

JOY IN FOLLOWING JESUS
Ria Lowing

"For I can do everything through Christ, who gives me strength."

Philippians 4:13 (NLT)

I was on the island of Lombok when the earthquake hit that place. Many people lost their houses and their families. I lived there for more than a year and helped give food and counseling for the victims. We would encourage and pray for them. During this situation, I felt what they felt too. I prayed to God and heard Him speak through the Word in Philippians 4:12. "I know what it is to be in need, and I know what it is to have plenty. I have learned the secret of being content in any and every situation, whether well fed or hungry, whether living in plenty or in want."

I learned from this to always be grateful in everything—through the good and the bad. Sometimes, we thank God only in good situations, not in the bad. God taught me many things through the situations I experienced in Lombok, and a lot of miracles happened. I met a woman who had been bleeding for 4 years, and we prayed together after I shared the story of when Jesus healed the woman who had been bleeding for 12 years. In 3 days, she got completely healed, and we continued learning about God's word. She even got baptized!

You can experience miracles, just like this woman did when you believe and pray in Jesus' name. "They replied, 'Believe in the Lord Jesus, and you will be saved, you and your household.'" Acts 16:31 When you decide to follow Jesus, your future is placed in His hands and you don't have to worry about it. He will give you true hope. You can see breakthroughs and healing in your life and family. God wants to use you as a tool to bring in souls for His glory, and the happiness that comes in that is more than if you were to win the lottery and win millions!

COMMON COMPASSION
Ben Lawalata

> "If a man has a hundred sheep and one of them gets lost, what will he do? Won't he leave the ninety-nine others in the wilderness and go to search for the one that is lost until he finds it?"
>
> Luke 15:4 (NLT)

We all have, probably more than a few times, witnessed an unexplainable evil, whether it was one that was committed to others or directly unto us. Either way, we all have to ask, how is one forgiven from that? Or, how does one forgive that? I've had my own share of experiences of not being able to forgive in my heart. My family's house was broken into one night that we were away. We got home to a complete mess, yet we didn't find anything missing except my electric guitar. It was my very first, and I knew that my dad had worked hard to get it.

That night, I felt violated and I was cursing the person responsible, praying that he would never see forgiveness. In response, God took me further into the situation and got me thinking that it could've been a lot worse. My family could've gotten hurt. How then would I forgive? Who gets to be forgiven? Why would Jesus forgive?

In Luke 15, Jesus speaks about redemption. Illustrating tax collectors and notorious sinners as a lost sheep, or a lost coin, or a lost son. Yes, the main theme here is that they're lost. In verse 4, Jesus asks this question: "Won't he leave the ninety-nine others in the wilderness and go search for the one that is lost until he finds it?" Jesus asks this as if this is a no-brainer. As if it was a common thing to do. Would you?

When someone is lost, they don't know a better way, otherwise they would not be lost. It's all they know, whether they've been misled or lied to. To them, that's all there is to know about life. So perhaps what we're asking here is not really the ability to forgive, but rather the ability to see as Jesus sees. That enables us to have the same compassion He has. To see past the evil deed and love the person no less. With the situation I had encountered, God enabled me to pray for the person instead, knowing that Jesus would go to search for him as He would to find me.

Faith Food Devotional

There's forgiveness. At the same time, God delivered me from having a life centered in sorrow.

If you're in a situation where you get to forgive, I'm writing this not just to ask that you would forgive. I pray that you will find the courage to do so. And find hope in Jesus, who through and in Him, we find perfect love that covers a multitude of sins. Mine, yours, theirs. Our hope is this: Jesus is enough. It's possible to forgive because we lack nothing in Him.

WHY WORRY WHEN YOU DON'T HAVE TO?
Rob Giles

"Therefore I tell you, do not worry about your life,
what you will eat or drink; or about your body, what you
will wear. Is not life more than food, and the body more
than clothes?"

Matthew 6:25 (NIV)

This is probably easier said than done. Life is just hard sometimes—maybe it has to do with our family, our spouse, a job, health issues, or for many it's about money matters. I admit that worrying is difficult to escape. Have we thought about how worry can even lead to physical health problems for us? As human beings, we want to avoid worry as much as the next person, but unfortunately, things don't work out the way we sometimes plan. Suddenly we might find ourselves in a place where we don't want to be and worry settles in. How do we overcome this? By completely trusting that Jesus is full of provision in everything.

I've witnessed His provision firsthand many times in my life when I didn't know how I was going to pay for something that was due or how I was going to get myself out of a situation I was in. In 2008, my family returned back to the United States after having spent four years serving as missionaries in China. The economy at the time was struggling, so my concern was how I'd find a suitable job to provide for my family, or even if I would find a job at all. As with all things, I brought this to the Lord in prayer because his promises are true, I knew that I could trust in Him, and He removed worry from my heart. Just shortly after returning to the states, God provided a good job for me that was enough to provide for my family, even in a bad economy. The God I serve is faithful. He knows what we need even before we ask in prayer.

God's timing is not always our timing, and we may try to look for the quickest answer to fix an issue, but His plans (which are good) might look different than yours. You don't have to trust in your own strengths and abilities. I encourage you to put into practice what the Bible teaches: give God your worry. Find peace and assurance that Jesus cares for every one of your needs. He knows exactly what you need when you need it.

Faith Food Devotional

CHECK YOUR PEACE
Becky Blanchard

"Do not be anxious about anything, but in everything by prayer and supplication with thanksgiving let
your requests be made known to God. And the peace of
God, which surpasses all understanding, will guard your
hearts and your minds in Christ Jesus."

Philippians 4:6-7 (ESV)

"Let the peace of Christ rule in your hearts, since as
members of one body you were called to peace. And be
thankful."

Colossians 3:15 (NIV)

You know those times in life where you know inside, something's
not right? You may not know why, or what exactly, but you have this
knowing inside. We have been made in the image of God, and according
to His likeness. In creation, something unique about humans is that we
have a body, a soul (which is our mind, will and emotions), and we have
a spirit. Our body will die one day, but our spirit, which is our true inner
self and how we truly connect to God, will exist forever. Through Jesus,
we have an unseparated connection to His Spirit. A lot of times, the
Bible refers to the heart: "Out of the overflow of the heart the mouth
speaks." Matthew 12:34 — and, "That the eyes of your heart would be
enlightened." Ephesians 1:18, and so on. Those scriptures aren't referring to our actual physical heart, but they are referring to our innermost
being. The heart, the innermost being, is where we really hear from God.

One time, my team and a few others were flying from Hong Kong to
India. My mom came to join us for that trip, and we had plans to minister in some children's homes that we were partnered with and at a boy's
prison in South India. After a super early morning start, we boarded our
plane, and my mom was seated next to me. As we were waiting for the
rest of the passengers to board, my mom got up to go to the bathroom.
After a good amount of time went by, she still hadn't come back. By this
point, they were making the announcements to take off and were closing the plane doors. I started to freak out! "Where in the world is Mom?"

I scanned the rows in front and behind and couldn't see her. Then I went to the back bathroom and still couldn't find her. I checked the front bathroom, she wasn't there either. I pulled a flight attendant aside and said, "Wait, we can't leave yet, I don't know where my mom is. She's missing!" I really started to panic thinking the worst, "Maybe my mom was abducted," and, "Who would want to take her?!" After pacing the aisles up and down searching every row, to my relief, I found her. There she was lying there in business class in one of the empty rows! This was an airline where there wasn't a distinct separation or difference between the business and economy class—except that the seats were bigger. "Mom, you freaked me out! I thought someone had taken you or something. The plane is about to take off and you didn't come back to your seat." My mom had just figured, "Hey, no one is sitting up here in business class. This is a long flight, I'm exhausted, so might as well." The flight attendant politely asked her to return to her seat with me. When she got back, I asked her, "Mom, what were you doing? You can't just go sit up in business class! And besides, you had me panicked!" "Becky," she replied, "Did you check your spirit?" (my heart). Although my actual heart was pulsing in frustration at that point, I did realize that even though I had no idea where she was, and even though what I saw was communicating the opposite of peace to my mind, I remember still feeling a peace deep inside my spirit. We laugh at that memory looking back at it today, but it was a valuable reminder.

131

God has given us His peace, and that has absolutely been one of the biggest signal guides in my life and journey: following the peace of God in my heart. That's how God wants to lead us. If we find anything besides peace "ruling in our hearts," then something needs to be reset. Don't let toxic emotions like anxiety, fear, anger, or depression rule your heart. Let it be His peace.

You can pray: "God, help me to be led by your peace, and may your peace always rule in my heart. Help me to recognize your peace when you're guiding me in the decisions and circumstances of my life. Amen."

MIRACLES

Taryon Crawford

> "Heal the sick, raise the dead, cleanse those who
> have leprosy, drive out demons. Freely you have
> received; freely give."
>
> Matthew 10:8 (NIV)

The first time I witnessed a miracle, other than my own, was while I was living in Cambodia. I went out with a team into a local village, and we met a man who had been deaf his whole life. As our team prayed for him, he began to hear about 5% (perfect hearing being 100%). We thanked God for opening his ears, and prayed about five more times for him until his hearing was 95% restored!

Jesus really is the Great Physician and His heart is to restore others to wholeness of body, soul, and spirit. What I learned from my experience seeing that man receive healing was this: persist in prayer, and take yourself out of the outcome of the prayer. It is the Father's will to heal. All we need to do is to be obedient to Jesus when praying for the sick.

LET GOD TAKE YOUR HAND
Donna Blanchard

"For I hold you by your right hand— I, the Lord your
God. And I say to you, 'Don't be afraid. I am here to help
you.'"

Isaiah 41:13 (NLT)

"For I hold you by your right hand." Remember when you were little
and your mom or another grown-up took your hand? Who was leading?
You or your mom? It was the grown-up because you couldn't see far
enough ahead. From a child's point of view, the world is just a bunch of
knees and feet!

Now your mom, on the other hand, could see far ahead and she
could navigate you to where you needed to go. I remember when I was
a little, I didn't want to hold my mom's hand in the grocery store and I
thought I was too big to sit in the cart. So, I held on to the cart instead.
I was walking along and, for a brief moment, I let go of the cart that my
mom was pushing. I got distracted, but then reached for the cart again.
I was walking down the aisle for some time and I glanced up to ask my
mom a question, but to my shock, it was not my mom! I had walked on
without looking up and attached myself to someone else's cart! Luckily,
it was a kind older woman. I looked frantically for my mom and found
her just where I had left her. I learned an important lesson that day.
Hold the hand of someone who knows more than you; don't wander off
and attach yourself to a stranger!

God says, "I'm here to help." God promises to guard you; to protect
and oversee, to watch from a high perspective. He will guard you from
your real enemy of your soul—the devil. He will take your hand when
you offer it and He is ready to lead you. He sees ahead and how to take
you through to the other side and guard you along the way.

Action: Offer your hand to God right now. Tell Him you are ready to
trust Him. He knows where you are going and how to get there. Don't
get distracted; it will only get you off track. Stay humble as you take
God's hand. There is protection there, and He will guard you. He will
take you by the hand and lead you and protect you. It is when you take
His hand that you realize you have never been alone.

Faith Food Devotional

ALWAYS ENOUGH
Stephen Walter

> "And my God will supply every need of yours accord-
> ing to His riches in glory in Christ Jesus."
>
> Philippians 4:19 (ESV)

An opportunity arose to go to El Salvador for a mission trip with the youth group from my church. This would be the farthest trip from home I had ever taken at the time. In the months prior to departure, the team prepared Gospel dramas, testimonies, and words of encouragement to share with the locals. It was on this trip that I met my current roommate serving with me in Bali, affectionately nicknamed "El Pepino," or "the Cucumber." For the majority of the trip, it proceeded as to be expected, with delicious tastes of the local cuisine, beautiful scenery of green mountains, and sharing the goodness of God with the locals.

As it came close to the end of our trip, we had one more site to go to. To all the different neighborhoods we had been visiting, we always brought with us packs of rice and beans to share with those in need. As this was the last site of our trip, we packed all we had left of our dwindling food supply, and brought it to the neighborhood. We set up our materials in the communal area and began playing music and games with the local children. A large crowd formed and gathered around to watch. We began counting all the adults who would, potentially, be receiving food, as well as double-checking the amount of our food supplies. As our main Gospel skit ended and El Pepino finished sharing the Gospel with the crowd, we called them to form a line to receive food. The line grew and grew to well over 100 people, but our excitement was stunted as the students who were tasked to count the food supplies reported that we only had 70 bags to give.

We decided to distribute what we could, and once we ran out, we'd apologize to the people and ask them to share. Then, one student spoke out in faith. He said that one bag should be grabbed at a time out of the larger bags while others prayed over the food. Eager anticipation arose within me as I thought, "Are we about to see a miracle?" The leaders decided to follow what the student had perceived to do, and one bag was handed out at a time while a team of students stood over the larger bags and prayed. I remember looking up and noticing that the line had grown with even more coming from their houses. I closed my eyes and said, "God, these are your people, and you will provide for them." One at a time, bag after bag was given, and the students never stopped praying over the food. The line finally began to shorten, and to our amazement, the food supplies were still coming out. It finally came to the last person in line. The team reached into the larger bag and pulled out the last bag of beans and rice and gave it. We all stood in awe of what had just happened. People stated that there was no way we had enough food for all those people, and yet there it was, we all saw it: God had provided just enough food for everyone. Our pastor was taken back. He sat down, took off his hat, and with a grin on his face he gently said, "Guys, we have just seen a miracle."

Before this miracle took place, most of us were willing to accept the reality of our situation because that is all we could see. It took the faith of one child to turn our minds back to God, and to remember we serve a God that does the impossible. Whether you are needing food, grace, forgiveness, or just encouragement, never accept the reality of what you see, but have faith that God is working in the unseen, and He will always provide.

OCEAN
Ricardo Rayon

> "That is what the Scriptures mean when they say,
> 'No eye has seen, no ear has heard, and no mind has
> imagined what God has prepared for those who love
> Him."
>
> 1 Corinthians 2:9 (NLT)

> "Commit everything you do to the Lord. Trust him,
> and he will help you."
>
> Psalm 37:5 (NLT)

I was in Bali, Indonesia and my friends and I went snorkeling in a beautiful place with a Japanese shipwreck. I think my last time snorkeling before that trip was like ten years before that. As I entered the water, I started to get nervous without knowing why. I didn't want to be far from the shore, but I also wanted to see what was in the ocean. So I told myself, "I can do this in the name of Jesus Christ." I felt God settle my spirit and I was able to control my nerves to go and explore. It was one of the most amazing trips I had ever been on!

I had always dreamed of going to the other side of the world to share the Good News, and when the opportunity to move to Asia presented itself, of course, I was excited, but also I felt stuck. I had no idea how it was going to happen. I remember one day I was walking in the street in my hometown, in Mexico, and I said to God, "Help me believe. I don't have enough money, I don't know exactly what activity I'm going to do in Asia, I have no home, and everything is unknown, but I believe you." God provided the money for a one-way plane flight. I took that flight, and since then, these years have been the best years of my life, and the best adventure of all.

When we walk with Jesus, somehow we know that everything is going to be ok, but we are also somehow cautious, especially to the unknown. Let me tell you, trusting in Him is the best adventure ever. God never disappoints and He never fails! He is extending an invitation to walk with Him in the unknown, to trust Him in every area of our life, surrender to Him, and follow His word. It's life's greatest adventure!

THE INGREDIENTS MAKE THE PRODUCT
Rodney Richard

"Since God chose you to be the holy people He loves, you must clothe yourselves with tenderhearted mercy, kindness, humility, gentleness, and patience. Make allowance for each other's faults, and forgive anyone who offends you. Remember, the Lord forgave you, so you must forgive others. Above all, clothe yourselves with love, which binds us all together in perfect harmony. And let the peace that comes from Christ rule in your hearts. For as members of one body you are called to live in peace. And always be thankful."

Colossians 3:12-15 (NLT)

When I bake a cake, I pay attention to the ingredients that I use. Are they fresh or out of date? Do they add to the process or take away from it? Do they make the cake taste better or bitter?

In my life, marriage, family, and ministry it is easy to overlook the importance of every ingredient. I can avoid hard conversations, get lazy with the important things, let things slip into my life that don't need to be there. I may think that they don't matter, but they do. The ingredients make up the final product. I'm "baking" for the King of Kings and I can't afford to cut corners, use bad ingredients or let bitterness settle into my life, family, marriage, or ministry. I'm "baking" for the King.

Pay attention to the small things every day. What you read and who you surround yourself with. Get rid of everything that is not a good ingredient, you are "baking" for the King!

KINDNESS
Fero Permatasari

> "Love never fails. But where there are prophecies,
> they will cease, where there are tongues, they will be
> stilled; where there is knowledge, it will pass away."
> 1 Corinthians 13:8 (NIV)

When I was a kid, I always admired love, and watching people who were "love do-ers". In other words, I loved seeing acts of love done for others, and seeing how it can change things. Even in terribly hard situations, love has given a reason for some people to survive. It makes me happy to think about all of the many people showing kindness and love, and about those who love without categorizing each other by race, background, or belief. When I worked at the hospital, I witnessed kindness and acts of love on a daily basis. I would see husbands constantly at their wife's side while she was giving birth, helping and supporting her. Or how the senior medical staff would give all their time to help others even though they had their own family. Even our work schedule hardly gave us any break times because we always had to be on call. This is love and kindness.

God teaches us the right kind of love because He is love. Love is not just a word, but an action. He does love us, and that's why He died for us. John 15:13 says, "Greater love has no one than this: to lay down one's life for one's friends." I once nearly gave up on my calling from God. But, through the revelation that He always loves me, and He has given, and always gives His all for me, I was reminded not to give up on Him. Since that revelation, I promised that I would never give up on love. He will always be there for us and He never gives up on us.

God teaches us, "'Love the Lord your God with all your heart and with all our soul and with all your mind.' This is the first and greatest commandment. And the second is like it: 'Love your neighbor as yourself.'" Matthew 22:37-39

We're all here because we're called to love. Instead of being suspicious of people or those who are different from you, why don't we love them and bring them closer to love. Let's be love do-ers. We're meant to be help people encounter the God of love through our lives.

TIME IS OF THE ESSENCE
Becky Blanchard

"For if you keep silent at this time, relief and
deliverance will rise for the Jews from another place, but
you and your father's house will perish. And who knows
whether you have not come to the kingdom for such a
time as this?"

Esther 4:14 (ESV)

"You are the light of the world. A town built on a hill
cannot be hidden. Neither do people light a lamp and
put it under a bowl. Instead, they put it on its stand, and
it gives light to everyone in the house. In the same way,
let your light shine before others, that they may see your
good deeds and glorify your Father in heaven."

Matthew 5:14-16 (NIV)

My dad has always prayed this prayer that has stuck with me to this
day: "God, help me to be in the right place, at the right time, speaking
the right words to the right people."

One year, when I was the outreach pastor at Sky City Church in Hong
Kong, I brought a team to Kathmandu, Nepal. We ministered there with
one of the local churches we were partnered with. It was December, so
we planned to do special Christmas programs in the different village
neighborhoods throughout the city. At one of the village areas we went
to, we looked for a space to set up our sound system and instruments
where the church could perform songs they wrote and where we could
do a couple of Christmas dramas that shared the Gospel message. We
found an open area right in the middle of the village. It was a perfect
location—except that it was where one of the oldest Hindu temples of
Kathmandu was located.

According to culture, it was only proper for us to seek out the elders
of that community to get their permission to be able to find the right
place for us to set up and have our program. We found them and spoke
with them saying that we had a Christmas program we would like to
share with the community. One of the elders pointed over to this plat-

form right in front of their temple and said, "We love Christmas programs. Here, you can present it right here." Although excited, we didn't know what their response would be when we finished everything, but we knew that good things were going to happen. We set up, and the local church team played their songs in Nepali and we sang some Christmas carols together. We finished the program with our Christmas drama presentations. Afterward, I went up to explain what they were watching in those dramas—God's gift of love for us in His Son, Jesus, who came to bring us back into a living, personal relationship with Him. Over 500 people gathered in that community area with some even watching from outside their windows and the front doors of their homes. Their hearts were so receptive and we felt the presence of God there.

140

We invited anyone forward who wanted to say yes to this gift from God, asking Jesus to be the leader of their life and who wanted to know Him better. One hundred eighty-one people came forward, and we got to lead them in a prayer of faith and give them Bibles that day! They were all invited to the local church by the members that were with us at that outreach. We later found out from the senior pastor that he and his outreach team have never been able to minister in that area because of how strongly set-in the Hindu peoples' traditions were. He shared how it was a miracle from God that we were allowed to even minister there, let alone right in front of the Hindu temple and that the message that was preached came from a woman. Culturally, it was not traditional for women to be in roles of public speaking, or in a position of community authority. Who knew! But we knew God was with us that day, and it was so cool to be a part of that miracle.

Fast forward four months later to the crazy earthquake of 2015 that hit Kathmandu. It devastated thousands in the community; many were displaced from their homes, and sadly, there were hundreds of deaths. I remember receiving a phone call from one of my local friends there. She was in a field and said it was so surreal watching these concrete buildings sway back and forth like they were made out of rubber. The buildings that had the most devastating damages were the ones that had been there the longest (having poorly-built structures). Most all of the old Hindu temples fit that description. I asked my friend about that one village and what had happened to that area. She told me, "Becky, the temple fell apart and was destroyed. That whole community and all their homes were completely devastated!" What a sobering realization of how significant that timing was for us to be there to share the Gospel. It was an appointed time and an appointed place to be there with those people.

God has an appointed place for you to be right now, and there is a message he's giving you to share that can bring His light to dark places. Why don't you ask God, "Lord, help me to recognize the appointed times I'm in—and to be in the right place, speaking the right words to the right people. Amen."

COMPASSION
Taryon Crawford

> "When he saw the crowds, he had compassion on them because they were confused and helpless, like sheep without a shepherd."
>
> Matthew 9:36 (NLT)

While living in Scotland, I went prayer walking with a friend and we came upon a huge crowd of Goth teenagers that were hanging out in a park. They were all drinking and doing drugs, and even though we got strange looks after approaching them, we made friends with a girl named Amanda. She began to tell us that many of the kids there had run away from home. These kids couldn't get into bars since they were under-age, so the park was the only place for them to hangout. I felt deep compassion for all of these young people, and we began to share about the love of the Father. My friend and I became big sisters for them. We would go back several times during the week to spend time with them to show them that they were thought about, and cared about. Eventually, we even invited them to eat with our friends. Through these small acts of kindness, two of the girls accepted Christ as their Savior, and they began sharing the same love they had received to the rest of their friends. Our Father in Heaven used us to reach an isolated community of teenagers who were lost and without hope during that time. God is love. He brings belonging, and acceptance, and He was exactly what these precious one's were looking for.

Jesus is the one who pours out His love in our hearts which compels us to share with others. When He pours out His love to you for someone else, take the next step to engage with those around you who desperately need to know how loved they are by our Father in Heaven.

SECRET TO SUCCESS
Ben Lawalata

"Seek the Kingdom of God above all else, and live righteously, and he will give you everything that you need."

Matthew 6:33 (NLT)

I really believe that if our devotion entries here were episodes for people to stream, this one would be among the most-clicked titles. It's a great catchphrase; besides, who wouldn't be intrigued about finding out the most solid way to success?! Here's some famous jargon pertaining to the topic that you might have heard often, "You can be successful like me!" Everybody wants to be successful. Is there a secret to it though? Or rather, the question should be along these lines: How do we know if we're successful? Would we want more if we are? Does it mean that we're not there yet if we still want to be more successful?

Have you ever talked to God about your dreams? What about your chances of getting rich? I have. In my conversation, God asked me what drives me toward success. It ended up with me realizing that, even more than the desire to be successful, I have fear of not being it, being successful. Because if I didn't succeed, I failed. If I didn't have success, then I'd have nothing. Then, God asked me, "If life is just either 1 or 0, success or not, then where does the rest of the life I've given you go? How would you be able to see my goodness? And if you can't see my goodness, how can you praise me? Without faith, how can you ever please me?"

It says in Psalm 53:2, "God looks down from heaven upon the sons of men, to see if there are any that are WISE, that SEEK after God." So there's the big reveal: there is wisdom in seeking after God, not after success. Seeking after God is your greatest success. His favor upon you is your greatest success in life.

Continuing the conversation, God then said to me, "Whatever it is that you do, I will bless it. Each step you make, I will bless every move, all the way through. You are who you are because of who I am." Isn't this a huge promise to receive? He is proclaiming that I'm always going to see success. God, He is able to do that. He can steer every area of my life and drive it into success. Maybe I won't see it right away, but He is

Faith Food Devotional

committed to bring me there. He is committed to being on the journey with me every step of the way. Should I then start a business and make money? If He says to go and do so, then yes. Will He bless it? Absolutely. But more than that, it's about being His child who does what the Father does. Psalm 32:8 says, "I will instruct you and teach you in the way you should go, I will guide you with My eye". Where His heart is, is where His children go. And His favor is upon them. That is their biggest success.

I might not know what you're going through right now, but here's a pointer to success: seek God above all else. Things may not seem like they're going your way, but if your way is His way, it will all work together for good. What you're doing will bless others, and you won't lack anything. Because God, the only one who is good, loves His children. He's with you. He keeps you, and He guides you, every step of the way.

MY PLANS AREN'T YOUR PLANS
Stephen Walter

"For I know the plans I have for you," declares the
Lord, "plans to prosper you and not to harm you, plans
to give you hope and a future."
Jeremiah 29:11 (NIV)

Have you ever built up an idea in your mind to such grand lengths? Like imagining your next birthday, or your wedding, and planning every little detail in your mind to perfection, but only coming to learn that nothing really works out the way you plan it? I know how that feels. I had built up the thought of my baptism to be a large event with all my family there to witness. I had always pictured myself in my church's baptism tank with my father and my pastor. Being able to look out and see all the smiling faces of my family and friends as I arose from the water seemed like it would be the pinnacle of my Christian journey. I wanted it to be so perfect that I had been procrastinating it until I felt the timing was just right; however, I learned that God had a different plan than mine.

I went on a mission trip to El Salvador. This trip was full of the spectacular and the miraculous as we shared the love of God with so many people. My favorite part though came at the end of our trip. We visited a beautiful black sand beach that was complemented by tide pools as large as hot tubs. The waves would crash against the rock and splash water in and out of the tide pools. As we were there, one of the leaders looked at me and asked if I had ever been baptized. I had never mentioned to anyone on that trip of my baptism plan, or even that I had never been baptized. The thought never crossed my mind that it could be today. The Holy Spirit had to have been speaking to her. I was taken back by her question, but answered honestly, "No, not yet." With a soft, but decisive tone, she asked me, "Why not today?" This wasn't how I had planned it, and I was hesitant to give an answer.

At that moment, I felt a strange wave of peace flood over me. Although I had wanted this special moment in my life to look the way I'd imagined it to, I could feel God telling me this was His timing. I mustered up my courage and replied, "Yep, let's do this." I made my way into the tide pool and saw everyone staring back at me, all with cheerful smiles. It was finally happening. The moment I had planned so differently in my head was at play. God saw my plans and turned them around into His will and timing so that I could see that He was, has been, and always will be in control. I arose from the water feeling an overwhelming sense of joy and freedom knowing that God saw me right where I was, and claimed me as a son.

You can create amazing plans that make all the sense in the world, but if you aren't willing to let them go for the sake of God's will upon your life, you could remain stuck in an endless loop of "what ifs". You don't have to give up all your hopes and plans for the sake of pursuing God's will. God has placed those plans in your heart for you to dream about and pursue, but you must trust God in the details. Remind yourself that His way is higher than yours, and His plans aren't always your plans. Do not lean on your own understanding, but in all your ways acknowledge him, and He will make your paths straight. (Isaiah 55:8-9, Proverbs 3:5-6)

HEARING GOD'S VOICE
Becky Blanchard

"But when He, the Spirit of truth, comes, he will
guide you into all the truth. He will not speak on His
own; he will speak only what he hears, and he will tell
you what is yet to come."

John 16:13 (NIV)

"My sheep hear my voice, and I know them, and they
follow me."

John 10:27 (ESV)

The most significant moment in my life that I can remember hearing God's voice for myself to guide me was when I was in high school,
either a junior or a senior. As my love for Jesus grew, I would dedicate
time to pray for the nations that I was learning about where many have
never heard of Jesus and there were great injustices. I think by my senior year, I knew that I wanted to go to Bible school and serve God in
full-time ministry, reaching people who didn't know Christ and being a
voice for those who had none.

I asked God to guide me and show me which Bible school I should
go to. There are a lot of great options out there, but which one did He
want me to go to? Some family friends of ours had attended Christ for
the Nations (CFNI) in Dallas, Texas, which is a Bible school that has
a big emphasis on world missions. I really felt the Lord highlight that
school in my heart over and over, even though I didn't know much about
it. I asked God to confirm somehow if that was for sure the one He was
leading me to. Shortly after, the director of CFNI was speaking at my
parent's Bible school in Mexico and asked what I wanted to do after
high school. After I told him, he invited me to consider coming to their
school and said that they would like to offer me a scholarship. Well, no
one knew about the prayer I said to God asking Him to confirm things,
but for me, that certainly was a confirmation and I felt more assurance
to go. I shared the news with my parents, and they were happy that
I heard from God. One thing I really appreciate about them is that in
each season as I was growing in my walk with God, they always taught

us kids that we could hear the voice of God for ourselves. However later that same year, we were hosting a team with us in Mexico. The leaders of that team were a couple who had made an impact on me in my high school years, and I really looked up to them. When the husband asked where I was planning to go and I told him, he responded, "No, that's not where you want to go. You want to come to the Bible school we're working at...that's the best fit for you." I was confused. I had looked up to them for years. I went to God in prayer asking, "God, what do I do?" I heard God ask my heart, "Have they been praying and seeking my guidance on where you should go? No, you have, Becky. That's what they think, but what did I tell you?" "Yeah, that's right, you spoke to me about going to CFNI," I responded in my heart. "Then, that's what you should do." he assured me.

At that point, I learned that even though there are others in our life that have advice and wisdom, the bottom line is that you can hear from God, and what is He telling you? In the end, what's most important is if we've followed God's voice in our lives. Sometimes we can go through hard seasons where our thinking might be unclear or in a state of dissolution, and in those times, it's especially important that we hear and listen to the advice of sound counsel. That's not what I'm talking about. I'm talking about learning to hear the voice of God for ourselves. He wants to guide us in a personal way, and it's not just the theologian or the pastor who has the unique privilege to hear from God. That's why Jesus came, and that's why He gave us the Holy Spirit, so we could learn to know Him better and hear Him for ourselves.

Ask Him now to help you to learn to recognize His voice more clearly. Holy Spirit, I need you and want to learn to recognize your voice in my life. Open my ears to hear you, and open my eyes to see what you want to show me in this season I'm in right now. Amen.

GOD SAW YOU IN YOUR MOTHER'S WOMB
Ismael Garza

"Before I formed you in the womb I knew you, before
you were born I set you apart; I appointed you as a
prophet to the nations."
Jeremiah 1:5 (NIV)

I remember the story that my mother told my twin brother and me about when she was pregnant with us. The doctor told my mother that she had a high-risk pregnancy because of the size of her two sons within her womb. After a few months of my mother being pregnant, the doctor called my parents to come in for an important meeting. The doctor told them that it could be possible that either their babies might die or that both my mother, brother and I could die. My mom shared with us about how scared she was, but as she arrived home after hearing the news, the only thing she knew to do was to pray to God. My mother said to God, "If these babies stay alive, it's because you have a purpose for their lives." She made a promise to God that if we came into the world, she would dedicate us to God and that we would serve Him.

The doctor sent my mom to be bed-ridden for 4 months during the pregnancy. She had to have her legs raised, and she had to be careful when she needed to go to the bathroom because of the risk of us coming out of her. Through this whole season, my mother put her trust in God. The surgery went well and my brother and I came out into this world healthy. Today I'm 29 years old and serving God in Asia, and my brother is a worship leader in the church.

I believe that God has an amazing plan for your life and it's going to come to pass no matter what situation you are in. Trust in Jesus, and don't give in to fear. Stand firm. God hears the prayers that your mother, your family members, or that others have prayed for you. God is going to fulfill His will in your life as you surrender yourself to Him. I hope this is an encouragement for you who are trusting for God's plans for anyone that you are praying for. Jesus hears your prayers.

Also, if you have a desire to have children, I want to encourage you that you can start praying for them now already! God is good all the time and the plans He has for you are good too!

Faith Food Devotional

MOVE THAT MOUNTAIN
David Blanchard

> "Then Jesus said to the disciples, 'Have faith in God.
> I tell you the truth, you can say to this mountain, 'May
> you be lifted up and thrown into the sea,' and it will
> happen. But you must really believe it will happen and
> have no doubt in your heart. I tell you, you can pray for
> anything, and if you believe that you've received it, it
> will be yours.'"
>
> Mark 11:22-24 (NLT)

One evening in Nuevo Laredo, Mexico, we were ministering with a church group from the United States. After the youth group performed dramas and some people shared their personal testimony of how God had changed their life, I headed over to prepare to distribute the beans and rice to these precious, humble people living in a one-room house made of cardboard and plywood. I was already exhausted from the heat and the ministry schedule for that week. I was ready to finish that evening's ministry site.

One of the team members, Paula, who also was a Spanish teacher, came over and said to me that the lady in the wheelchair wanted someone to pray for her. This was Imelda, who attended the mission when her husband allowed her to come. She'd had Parkinson's disease for the last five years. I sent Pastor Manuel with Paula to go pray for her as I got ready for the food distribution. The youth pastor, Joey Rumble, was helping me when Paula came back and said that the lady wanted someone else to pray for her. I told her that I was sure if God wanted to heal Imelda right then, that he would have done so when the pastor prayed for her. Paula was also a friend of mine, and grabbed my shirt collar and said firmly, "Brother David, the lady wants someone else to go pray for her!" "OK, I'll go with you," I replied. After greeting Imelda, I knelt down in front of her wheelchair and said with a half-hearted voice, "So let's pray." As I prayed, the Holy Spirit said to me, "Imelda has faith that I can heal her. What about you?" Wow, I realized that this woman was fervently praying and believing that God was going to heal her and move this mountain of Parkinson's disease right out of her life!

I was just mumbling a few words in my prayer. I said, "Hey everyone, let's really pray with faith!" So Paula, Pastor Manuel, Victor, myself, and others begin to pray. The Lord said to me, "How many times have I said, 'Woman, your faith has made you whole!'" I said, "Imelda, do you have faith that God can heal you?" She said, "Oh yes, Brother David!" I then said, "Then rise up and walk in the name of Jesus Christ!"

Imelda had been confined to the wheelchair for many years. Her husband, or son, had to move her to do whatever she needed. Now, she was standing and Paula was on one side of her holding her up and I was on the other side. I said, "Let's walk." Imelda begins taking baby steps. We begin to help her walk by holding her up at first. She began to take little steps and then bigger ones until she was walking. There were about 180 people watching us as they were waiting to receive rice and beans from the distribution line. They were wondering what in the world we were doing with Imelda. "She can't walk—she has Parkinson's!"

Then the Holy Spirit said to me, "RUN!", so I said, "Imelda, Paula, let's run!" We began to walk faster and faster and then we began to run. I told Paula, "Let go of her!" and Imelda took off running all over the field! The sun had set and now only the full moon was shining on the field. The people waiting in the line for the food distribution immediately ran over and said, "Hey, please pray for me! Pray for me!" The team began to pray together with us and people got touched by the power of the Holy Spirit! The wind began to blow and the people were anointed by the Holy Spirit. Some were kneeling down and others were overcome by God's presence as God was moving the mountains of many people's problems and situations in their lives. Some fell down and were lying on their backs praying. Later that night, we finally distributed the beans and rice. Everyone was blessed. Imelda pushed her wheelchair home! Her son gave his life to Christ also and became a believer in God.

There's a Christian song that says we should "only believe, only believe, for all things are possible if we only believe." We must speak to the mountains in our life, the situations, the circumstances, the problems, the needs, and believe that God is great enough to handle every one of our needs according to His divine plan. We must trust in God and put our faith in Him and believe for the impossible. Today is the day for your miracle, and God is waiting for you to put your faith in action and believe in him!

151

YOU ARE ENOUGH

Chantel Garza

> "I thank Christ Jesus our Lord, who has given me strength, that he considered me trustworthy, appointing me to His service."
>
> 1 Timothy 1:12 (NIV)

A lie that many of us can believe is: "What if what I do or give isn't enough in the eyes of the Lord?" This is a lie I have certainly believed, and it's something that the Holy Spirit highlighted in my life while being in ministry. I questioned whatever I did, wondering if it was enough. This robbed me of my joy, and robbed me of the knowledge of how accepted and pleasing I am to Jesus already. But this is the truth: What I do for him and who I am in His eyes is enough.

Even if all we've said is "YES!" to Him, and have been obedient to what He has asked us to do, He is already pleased! Just being who He has created us to be, His children, brings much joy to Him. I found that when I was living life through that lie that I was believing, I would unknowingly be cursing what Jesus had already given me instead of being thankful, surrendering it to Him, and asking Him to bless it and help me. You can bless or curse what you have been given by Jesus through the words you say over yourself and over what He has given you (your gifts and talents).

When Jesus held the five loaves and two fish, He didn't see what He was given as not enough. Instead, He raised it to His Father, asked that He would bless it, and it multiplied to be more than enough for God's purpose that day. So as we acknowledge this lie in our lives, we can repent and again thank Jesus for what He has given us (our giftings, abilities, talents, personalities). Surrender it all to Jesus, and ask Him to bless what you have to overflow and to give Him glory. Know that what you do and who you are is enough for the purposes to which He has called you to. Make this truth secure in you!

Application: Take time to ask the Holy Spirit to reveal any lies you may be believing (in relation to this devotion). Bring it before the Lord and repent for believing these lies, and ask Jesus to help you to know where they came from. Let the Holy Spirit minister to you. Once you know where the root of the lie came from, ask the Lord to reveal His truth to you so you can replace the lies with the truth. Use His word (which is His TRUTH) as a weapon the next time you hear the lies. YOU ARE ENOUGH AND WHAT YOU DO FOR THE LORD IS ENOUGH!

153

GIVE IN FAITH
Vanessa Birkbeck

> "And my God shall supply all your needs according to
> His riches in glory by Christ Jesus."
>
> Philippians 4:19 (NKJV)

We have all been affected in some way during the recent global Coronavirus pandemic. Many of us have been isolated in our homes and not able to travel or do ministry like we normally do, and on top of that, we have also seen reduced financial support to continue the work. But God always comes through to encourage us to continue pressing into Him as our source for everything. We have been so grateful for generous donations and gifts given to our ministry by the faithful, even during this time of isolation, shortages and separation.

I am reminded of when Paul wrote his letters to the Philippians when he was in isolation in one of the worst prisons in the Roman Empire. Paul was restricted in every way—locked up and unable to make any money or have even the basic comforts of everyday life. Then, he received a special financial offering that came by hand in a letter from the church of Philippi where he had been ministering. Because Paul was a Roman citizen, this monetary gift could be put into a special account, but could not be accessed by him until he was released. It was more than the value of the gift itself. It was that the church had confidence in him and was praying and believing in faith that when released, he would have funds to continue in society and in his ministry. In faith, the Philippian Christians, knowing that he would need support when he was set free, were believing and preparing for that day. This faith action brought great encouragement to Paul. He wrote back to the Philippian church that God would supply all their needs because of their giving in faith (See Philippians 4:19).

Likewise, the gifts received into the ministry have brought great encouragement to our ministry team! It is much more than the monetary value of the gifts. It is seed sown in faith in this season of closure and restrictions, for us to continue to mentor the nations, extending our reach and use every opportunity to preach the Gospel when the pandemic restrictions are finally lifted. If we are givers or have given in faith, just as the Philippian church did, we can also pray this scripture knowing that God shall supply even more abundantly! Our God, who has no limitations, no restrictions, no lack, no shortage is more than sufficient in everything! When we give to God's Kingdom, He will meet our needs and unlock heaven's resources even to the point of overflowing!

Let's Pray: Father, I thank You for this encouragement today. Your word says that You shall supply all of our needs according to Your riches in glory by Christ Jesus. So, we stand on Your promise knowing that, as we give to Your Kingdom, You will meet and abundantly supply all of our needs. I pray this in Jesus' name and for His glory. Amen.

THE SUN WILL COME UP AGAIN

Ricardo Kanter

> "The Lord's unfailing love and mercy still continue,
> Fresh as the morning, as sure as the sunrise."
>
> Lamentations 3:22-23 (GNT)

> "Israel, put your hope in the Lord, for with the Lord
> is unfailing love and with him is full redemption. He
> Himself will redeem Israel from all their sins."
>
> Psalm 130:7-8 (NIV)

> "In him we have redemption through His blood, the
> forgiveness of sins, in accordance with the riches of
> God's grace."
>
> Ephesians 1:7 (NIV)

I've been a Christian for ten plus years. I've been born again, I graduated from a Bible school, and I have heard the word "redeem" millions of times—but I never understood it until a difficult situation happened. My relationship with God became somewhat systematic. I prayed or read my Bible because I had to minister, and I lost connection. Little by little, I became more permissive in my way of living, and ministry became a job and not a lifestyle. I made several bad decisions, and one day, in a moment of worship, I couldn't take it anymore and I exploded. I confessed everything wrong that I had done and exposed my heart, first before God, and then before my team, pastor, and family. I was so sad that I had damaged my relationship with God and I was afraid that it would be extremely difficult to get it back. I was afraid of the consequences, that God would reject me, and that I would be humiliated.

My soul was very sad and in fear, and my only consolation was to read Psalms. I identified so much with the Psalms—specifically Psalm 130. Every time I read it, I experienced an overwhelming sense of peace. In that Psalm, I recognized a particular word, "redemption." It means: "The action of saving or being saved from sin, error, or evil and regaining or gaining possession of something in exchange for payment, or clearing a debt." It was the first time in all my years of following Jesus that I understood the meaning of redemption. It was the first time I understood that my debt IS PAID! Immediately my feelings of sadness and fear were gone, and instead, I experienced love, peace, and joy.

Redemption is real. All of us who confess Jesus' name and believe in our hearts are saved. I love what it says in Romans 10:11, "Anyone who believes in him will never be put to shame." He is a good father and a faithful master.

I want to encourage you that exposing your heart to God is worth it. Let him penetrate the darkest parts of your heart so that He can bring freedom, peace, or whatever you need, right where you are. Take a few minutes to talk to your Father; Receive His redemption and have faith that no matter the situation, He will not abandon you or humiliate you.

BEAUTIFUL FEET
Donna Blanchard

> "And how will anyone go and tell them without being
> sent? That is why the Scriptures say, "How beautiful are
> the feet of messengers who bring good news!"
>
> Romans 10:15 (NLT)

When I look at my feet, I mean really look at them, I think they are
so funny looking. Have you ever gathered in a circle to pray and you
look at everyone's feet? They are so different, and honestly I think feet,
especially toes, are kind of ugly.

In 2012, my husband and I were preparing to go on a trip to Nepal
and meet our daughter Becky, who serves as a missionary in Asia. One
week before my trip, I was moving a large piece of furniture. I dropped
it on my big toe. Pain shot from my toe all the way up my leg. I looked at
my toe at the base of the toenail; it was bleeding profusely and throbbed
with every beat of my heart. I immediately grabbed my foot and began
to pray.

This was not the first time I had injured my toenail or a fingernail.
I knew by experience that it would take weeks for my toe to be fully
healed. I was leaving for Asia in just one week! I began to pray and pray
over my toenail. I began to speak to it to be healed in Jesus' name. I declared over it that I would not lose the toenail. For the next 10 minutes,
my toe throbbed. I spoke again to my toe to be healed, and soon the pain
began to subside. Within one hour it stopped hurting completely. I went
to bed (as it was late) and I woke up with a completely healed toenail!
Now, the story doesn't end there. Fast forward two weeks, my husband
David and I are in Nepal with Becky and her team from Wings. Her team
had been ministering to a group of street boys, and we had gathered
them in a park for lunch, played soccer together, and ministered the
Gospel to them. The boys did not have shoes—only a few had flip flops.
During our time of soccer, one of the young boys (who was a kind of
one of their leaders) kicked the soccer ball so hard that his toenail on
his big toe was completely torn off except that it was hanging there
by a small piece of skin. We stopped to wash his feet and clean up the
toe as we were praying. I told him the story of how God had healed my

toenail and that God would heal his toes too! I put a band-aid on it, and we had lunch. As we were leaving the park he called me over, he said, "Mom, look at my toe!" He took the band-aid off and his toenail was reattached like nothing had ever happened! Then he told me it did not hurt at all.

The toe doesn't seem to be an important part of the body, but without it we lack great balance. In Bible times, if you did not have a thumb or big toe you were not useful in battle. Without a big toe, your balance would be off and you could not run after the enemy. So the next time you look at your dirty, stinky old feet, remember, God says your feet are beautiful, and He wants to use your feet to bring good news to others.

159

REFLECT
Becca Giles

> "But whenever someone turns to the Lord, the veil is
> taken away. For the Lord is the Spirit, and wherever the
> Spirit of the Lord is, there is freedom. So all of us who
> have had that veil removed can see and reflect the glory
> of the Lord. And the Lord—who is the Spirit—makes
> us more and more like him as we are changed into His
> glorious image."
>
> 2 Corinthians 3:16 (NLT

During a time of worship, I opened up my hands, and I saw a picture of Jesus put a beautiful box in them. I opened up the box and pulled out what looked like a necklace of prisms. I realized it was a crown, and I put it on my head. I heard the Lord say, "Becca, your life is going to reflect my Kingdom."

His Kingdom is full of righteousness, peace, and joy in the Holy Spirit (Romans 14:17).

Years later, I had been hurt by an instance that happened with a classmate of mine. We were no longer close friends, but I became aware that I was holding on to a lot of bitterness toward this person. In that moment, God showed me a picture of my heart on the inside—it was full of grim, heavy-looking rocks. One by one He helped me forgive every incident with this person that I could think of, and simultaneously, He took out each rock and replaced it with a prism. He said over me, "Becca, your heart can reflect my Kingdom."

The last one of these prism encounters I had was during a season in my life where I was living with "double vision"—but not with my natural eyes. Here's what I mean: I believed what the Word said about who I am in Christ; but at the very same time, I overly heeded the opinion of the world that says I must be a certain way to be good enough. My perception was skewed.

One morning, as I looked at myself in the mirror with my natural eyes, I legitimately began to see in double vision. There were two of everything around me, including two images of myself looking back at me in the reflection. I sensed that God wanted to speak to me through it, so

I researched and found this: A way to repair double vision if you have it, is to wear specifically designed glasses with prisms in the lenses.

So in a sense, my worldly perspective needed to refocus through a lens that first sees God's truth and then also believes that which is in His Kingdom. By doing that, that's when I will reflect His Kingdom through my life here on earth.

Whatever it is in you that's stopped looking very much like righteousness, peace, and joy, can be renewed. Nothing is too set in stone that it cannot be transformed when looking into the face of Jesus. What is it that you have focussed in on that needs to be re-focussed back onto Him? Your life on earth begins to reflect Jesus, even without mustering it up in your own strength, as you simply turn your attention on Him, and you just begin to behold Him.

CALLING TO GO
Fero Permatasari

> "Don't be afraid, from now on you will fish for people."
>
> Luke 5:10 (NIV)

> "What no eye has seen, what no ear has heard, and what no human has conceived the thing God has prepared for those who love Him."
>
> 1 Corinthians 2:9 (NIV)

Jesus died on the cross for everyone on this earth, restoring the broken relationship between humans and their Creator God. He has commanded us to go, to share the Gospel, and He will come back to earth when everyone has heard about it. It says in Matthew 22:14 that, "Many people are called, but few are chosen."

Who is going to tell the world about this news? Who wants to do it? Some people would say 'yes, but maybe later.' Some might ask, "How do I do it?"

When I was working in the hospital, I loved it so much. Every aspect of it brought me joy. I loved building relationships with the patients and being able to share stories and words of encouragement. I was walking one night, and one of my patients even recognized my footsteps as I walked down the hall. I used to love singing and dancing for my patients, and I would notice their beautiful smiles and happy laughter as I entered their room. In my first year at the hospital, I met a lady who suffered from a mental disorder, and she gave birth to a healthy baby boy. She came back again two years later to give birth, and despite her condition, she immediately recognized me. Working at this hospital gave me some of my most cherished memories, but after 5 years I had a feeling that things would be changing to something new. God told me that my current contract would be my last contract with this hospital. I was shocked and I cried because I didn't know what would happen next, but I said 'YES' to Him anyway. When we leave everything behind for everything He wants us to do, it's worth it. It isn't always comfortable, but God will always give you peace during the transition. AMEN.

WINGS INTERNATIONAL

God can use anyone and anything for His work on this earth, but He wants you to be part of it. No matter what you do, what season in life you are in, or what you have in life, God's great desire is for you to be part of His Kingdom. He is not checking your bank account, He is checking your faith. Keep holding on to Him, He is the one that we can surrender to. He knew you before you were born (Jeremiah 1:5).

Let's pray: Father in Heaven, help me to believe that you have a plan for my life. No matter where you are going to take me, help me to believe that you always lead me. I want to say 'yes' to you. I want to say 'amen' to everything ahead that comes from you. Thank you for being faithful to me, and for looking after me. I don't always know where to go, but I know you are leading me, Lord. Help me, Father. Amen.

163

PRAY FOR RAIN (OR NOT)
Becky Blanchard

> "Therefore confess your sins to each other and pray
> for each other so that you may be healed. The prayer of
> a righteous person is powerful and effective. Elijah was a
> human being, even as we are. He prayed earnestly that it
> would not rain, and it did not rain on the land for three
> and a half years."
>
> James 5:16-17 (NIV

One of my favorite things I've heard Reinhard Bonnke say (who was an amazing evangelist God used in Africa) was, "Man can do nothing without God, but God chooses to do nothing without man." It's so amazing how God includes us and He wants us to be a part of bringing His purposes to pass on this earth, together building the realities of His kingdom. Growing up working in Mexico with my parents, I got to see firsthand God do many miracles through His sons and daughters as we set out on His purposes on His mission. I can remember one time (I think I was 12 or 13 years old) when we were in Torreon, Mexico, and we had invited the village community together at this central soccer court area. Close to the time that we were going to have our ministry program, these dark, massive storm clouds began to gather overhead and cover the meeting place

I remember my dad got us together, and we all began to pray asking God to hold the clouds. Then we spoke with authority over the storm clouds and told them they had to wait until we were done. There were a bunch of teenagers on that trip from Uvalde, Texas, as well as my parents' ministry staff. We were all agreeing and praying fervently for this rain to be held so that people would have the opportunity to hear about Jesus and actually encounter Him in a real and personal way. The next thing I remember is that the storm clouds over us started to separate to where this tiny blue sky spot formed above us. The clouds kept parting, and the blue sky view kept getting larger and larger. Next thing you know, the sky directly over us was entirely blue, even though the storm clouds were still circled around the rest of the village area. It was such a cool sight to see!

Then in Bali, we have our kids' outreach program at the beach every Wednesday night. These nights have been our key nights in sharing the Gospel with them and their parents. In Bali, rain is very common, and especially in the rainy seasons, we are known to have unpredictable and heavy rainstorms that hit at a moment's notice. Each outreach night, we have always prayed for clear skies. And amazingly, in the history of over four years of ministry here, we can count on maybe one hand the times it has rained on those nights. Even on days that had been rainy and stormy the entire day, we would pray and when it came to the evening—nothing, no rain. It would stop!

165

You don't have to be a pastor, a Bible teacher, or a long-time believer in Jesus for your prayers to be significant or answered. Where you're at now, you can pray from your heart and things will happen! Is your heart right with God? If yes, ok, pray in faith. If not, get right with God. He gave everything to make this a possibility for you through Jesus. Ask God to help remove from you any hindrance from experiencing the fullness of His blessings in your life. There are also times that we can become so complacent in what we know to be true (having heard it so many times at church or from sermons) that we need to stir our hearts to press in and actually engage our faith when we pray.

Whatever point in your faith you find yourself today, know that your prayers matter and they are powerful and effective!

TURBULENCE
Ricardo Rayon

> "Do not be anxious about anything, but in every
> situation, by prayer and petition, with thanksgiving,
> present your requests to God. And the peace of God,
> which transcends all understanding, will guard your
> hearts and your minds in Christ Jesus."
> Philippians 4:6-7 (NLT)

> "Teach these new disciples to obey all the commands
> I have given you. And be sure of this: I am with you
> always, even to the end of the age."
> Matthew 28:20 (NLT)

Because of the ministry I have served with for several years now, I have had the opportunity to travel to many different countries. I remember I was in the Tokyo airport, waiting to take a flight to Hong Kong. When I was waiting at the gate, I had this impression from God: "Ricardo do you trust in me?" I said yes. I heard again, "Ricardo, do you trust in me?" Again I said yes. I heard the same question again before the plane took off. My answer was, "Yes, Lord!" A few minutes after being in the air, we experienced bad turbulence. It felt like a rollercoaster as everyone on the plane screamed, including myself. I was scared, but in those seconds I said, "God, I trust in you." Then I fell asleep. After a few hours of flying, we landed safely in Hong Kong. That season in my life felt like turbulence. I had no house, I was living on a different friend's couch, I didn't have enough financial supporters, and didn't have enough money in general. All I knew was that God had told me to be in Hong Kong and that He doesn't lie. So after those months of "turbulence" and learning to trust and believe in Him, I could learn more about myself and who my God is. Months later, I was given the largest donation I'd ever received. God is faithful.

It doesn't matter how bad your situation is, or how bad the "turbulence" is, God is with you. You are going to reach God's destiny for your life. All you need is to trust in Him. Cry out to Him, and He will answer you. He said, "Surely I am with you always, to the very end of the age."

PROTECTION DURING PERSECUTION
Ria Lowing

"I took you from the ends of the earth, from its
farthest corners I called you. I said, 'You are my servant,
I have chosen you and have not rejected you.' So do not
fear, for I am with you; do not be dismayed, for I am your
God. I will strengthen you and help you; I will uphold
you with my righteous right hand."

Isaiah 41:9-13 (NIV)

During my ministry on an island in Indonesia called Lombok, my
team and I experienced persecution from a group of Muslims who were
living there. They even tried to harm us several times, once by damag-
ing the tires of my leader's car. Praise God, we're all safe because God is
on our side. He was always looking after me and my team. Once, I was
in my own home and I felt that someone was following me in my house.
I was very scared because I was living alone in that house, and my team
was in another house. I prayed, and God strengthened me through what
it says in Isaiah 30:15. "Only in returning to me and resting in me will
you be saved. In quietness and in trust shall be your strength."

After I prayed, I received new strength and believed that God protected me even though I was alone at home. Even the persecution I experienced did not make me afraid to preach the word of God. I felt more
courageous because I knew the Spirit of God was in my heart, making
me brave. Every morning before I began my activities, I always took the
time to read God's word and pray for His protection.

After my team and I experienced that persecution, God honed in our
focus to the right group of people out of everyone that we had been dis-
cipling, and one month later, we saw many people receive Jesus as their
savior. We baptized more than ten people at that time. There are always
victories that will occur after persecution. Among the other things that
I experienced in Lombok, there was an attack from the enemy that tried
to make me feel that I was not worthy to serve God. But, even though
many things were difficult for me to go through in my ministry, I never
became disappointed in God.

I declared what it says in Isaiah 41:11-13 over all I did in my ministry. "All who rage against you will surely be ashamed and disgraced, those who oppose you will be as nothing and perish. Though you search for your enemies, you will not find them. Those who wage war against you will be as nothing at all. For I am the Lord your God who takes hold of your right hand and says to you, Do not fear; I will help you." Just as what is written there in God's Word happened in my life when I declared it.

168

Persecution or problems can come from those closest to us or from those on the outside. Always have a heart that is quick to forgive, just as the Father forgives you. I learned to forgive those who have hurt me, and I have joy and peace in my heart. When you are sure of your calling, continue to follow God's voice, obey Him, and don't be afraid of what he's called you to do. God has chosen you, and He will guide, strengthen, help, and even hold your right hand and say to you: "Don't be afraid."

LANGUAGES OF LOVE
Ismael Garza

"Dear friends, let us love one another, for love comes
from God. Everyone who loves has been born of God and
knows God."

1 John 4:7 (NIV)

We would travel every Sunday to Tuesday as a team to the village
in the north side of Bali. We have a community center there where we
share the Gospel to the children and families that live there through
English classes, sports, dance, and music. We have formed many friend-
ships with the families that live there surrounding our center, but in
this devotion, I want to share with you what Jesus did through one man
who lived right next to our center. Every week when we went up to the
center, we would spend time with him. He loved coming over. He loved
to sit outside our center for hours, and it brought him so much joy and
peace. We called him Guru Security. Guru means teacher, and we chose
the name "Security" because he always protected our center.

I didn't know how to share the Good News with him because of the
language barrier, but I didn't allow this to stop me from connecting with
him. I would sit near him, and little by little, he started trusting me. The
only thing I thought to do was to start giving him massages on his back
because I noticed he had pain and he was older. In his younger years,
he would work so hard in the field as a farmer and did construction as
well. So, every time I saw him, I chose to show the love of Jesus through
massaging him and using the best Indonesian I knew how to speak.

After 6 months of knowing Guru Security, he asked us about Christmas and what it meant. With the help of our local Indonesian friend
interpreting, this opened the door for us to share the full Gospel from
the beginning of creation to Jesus's death and resurrection. It was that
day that Guru Security gave his life to Jesus. He asked if he now had
to give any sacrifices or do any certain prayers, but we explained that
Jesus just wanted his heart and didn't require any certain ceremonies,
sacrifices or prayers. We know that he encountered Jesus that day. Just
3 months after, he died of sickness in his old age. But now we know he

is with Jesus!

LOVE is a powerful weapon that we have. It's a weapon that can be used beyond language. No matter what, love is always going to win. If you are unable to share the love of Jesus through words because of fear of your safety or language barriers, remember that your actions (filled with love) reflect the heart of Jesus. Don't give up! I pray that whoever God has brought along your path, as you choose to love them, that a door of opportunity will be made available for them to hear the Gospel!

DON'T WORRY
Fero Permatasari

"Ask and it will be given to you; seek and you will
find; knock and the door will be opened to you."
Matthew 7:7 (NIV)

Do you ever worry about anything? One night, I remember being
so overwhelmed with work and life that I felt extremely heavy in my
spirit. I prayed and brought my situation before God. In that moment,
I felt the hand of God hold my hand, and I heard His voice say, "Everything is going to be alright." That night, I learned how to focus on God's
perspective over my own worry and stress. Instead of remaining overwhelmed, I chose to pray and bring my burdens before the Lord. I was
filled with such gratitude towards God's lovingkindness in meeting and
comforting me. From my experience, it seems to me that there are two
types of people: those who are always grateful for everything, and those
who feel they never get enough. Which one are you?

For a long time, I was the latter. I used to live with a "lifestyle is followed by income" mindset. But let me tell you a secret: we can't always
get everything we need, but we can still be grateful for everything we
have.

There was a time in my life where I worried about a lot of things—
finances, gaining acceptance from people, having confidence in myself,
and the new seasons of life I would be facing in the future. I prayed and
thought about those things all the time. I was trying to manage it by
myself and with what I had. I realized that only gratefulness would help
me feel better.

Many times God spoke to my heart and reminded me of this verse
in Matthew 7:7.

I began asking Jesus for everything that I needed. Every single detail
that I had in my mind, I put it in my prayer. Days passed by, and I began
to realize that I had received everything I prayed for. I have it now! He
loves it when we are grateful and He still allows us to ask Him for more.
Always be grateful for every single thing you can think of that you have:
friends, relationships, your job, etc, because you always have enough.
Remember, we're His children, and we can ask anything to our Father.

Faith Food Devotional

He gives you more than enough.

Let's pray. Lord, please forgive me for my doubt and worrying. Help me to be even more grateful for every single thing. I believe that I have everything I need.

Bible verse declaration: "Therefore I tell you. Whatever you ask for in prayer, believe that you have received it, and it will be yours." Mark 11:24 (NIV)

YOU ARE RUNNING A RACE!
Chantel Garza

> "Do you not know that in a race all the runners run,
> but only one gets the prize? Run in such a way as to get
> the prize. Everyone who competes in the games goes
> into strict training. They do it to get a crown that will
> not last, but we do it to get a crown that will last forever.
> Therefore I do not run like someone running aimlessly;
> I do not fight like a boxer beating the air. No, I strike
> a blow to my body and make it my slave so that after I
> have preached to others, I myself will not be disqualified
> for the prize."
>
> 1 Corinthians 9:24-27 (NIV)

What are you crying out to Jesus for at this time? Do you trust that He is hearing your prayers and knows your heart's desires? I want to encourage you that no matter what place you find yourself in today— whether you're in a good season, a dry season, or a season filled with uncertainty—you are still in the race!

In today's scripture, I would like to highlight some things.

It is wonderful to know that Jesus has called us as His children and that we can be in relationship with Him, but will you do what He asks you to do and do it for Him, knowing that He sees you, He loves you, and He trusts you? How do we stay in this race till the end? How do we not give up? This has often been my question: "Jesus, how do I finish the race well and give you glory to the very end?" I need to run with a victorious mindset.

Jesus desires that we run victoriously in all areas of our lives! Here are some things to remember:

First thing, you are running a race with Jesus. Jesus is right next to you! Sometimes you will just be walking or running, but no matter what, Jesus is next to you and you are still in the race. Live today choosing again to be aware of His presence with you. No matter what, don't give up! Jesus is your personal cheerleader. God calls us in His Word to be courageous and to not give up. He is with us.

Second, stay in your lane. Do not take your eyes off of Jesus and compare your race with theirs. Comparison that is not dealt with can lead to jealousy and feelings of not being enough, or that what you have to give isn't enough. If you feel this way now, I want you to take the time to recognize these lies and repent from accepting them. Grab onto Jesus' truth about you. To run victoriously, we have to learn to hide in Jesus instead of hiding in the destructive patterns or lies that take us away from His truth for us. Your gift is what is needed in the church. We are all different parts of the body. The nose cannot be the head, and the nose needs the head to function as a whole. See yourself as Jesus sees you. If you desire this change in you, start praying and asking Him to open your eyes to this.

174

Third, throw off anything that stops you from running. Throw it off! If you have something against a brother or sister, don't gossip, but rather forgive them and talk to them. If your heart is struggling with something, run to Jesus with it, seek help, and talk to someone about it. Don't keep sin and lies hidden. Jesus desires us to run as children living in His fullness with no excess weight holding us back.

Lastly, run after Jesus' ways, His heart, His character. He is your coach, He is everything, and He is for you.

BIGGER BETTER
Rodney Richard

"What causes fights and quarrels among you? Don't
they come from your desires that battle within you? You
desire but do not have, so you kill. You covet but you
cannot get what you want, so you quarrel and fight. You
do not have because you do not ask God. When you ask,
you do not receive, because you ask with wrong motives,
that you may spend what you get on your pleasures."

175

James 4:1-3 (NIV)

When my kids were in high school and would have a birthday party,
we would play this game called 'Bigger and Better'. We would group the
kids up, give them a penny, and send them out into the neighborhood to
knock on our neighbors' doors to ask them to trade them for something
Bigger or Better. They would have an hour to keep trading up. They ended up bringing some incredible things back to the house (a TV, skill saw,
ping pong table, a couch). They just operated in a spirit of expectancy.
They were bold enough to ask someone to trade them for what they had
for something Bigger or Better.

I wonder what would happen if we were to live this way? Bold ask-
ers and generous givers! The game always needed both; someone bold
enough to ask the "Big Ask," and someone generous enough to give up
something for someone else. The key was the question: "What could be
possible if we were bold enough to ask big questions or bold enough to
give generously?"

Prayer: God, check our motives, give us bold hearts to ask You for
BIG things, and make us willing to respond BIG to the request of others.

GO THROUGH THE WAVE
Becky Blanchard

> "When you pass through the waters, I will be with
> you; and when you pass through the rivers, they will not
> sweep over you. When you walk through the fire, you
> will not be burned; the flames will not set you ablaze."
>
> Isaiah 43:2 (NIV)

Anybody who has swum in the ocean knows what it's like to experience waves, constantly crashing on the shore and against you when you walk through them. Waves are powerful forces of nature, and when stuck on the wrong end of them, can be pretty dangerous. When a giant wave comes at you the best idea is not to swim away from it, but rather face it and swim through it. One time in Bali (where our base is), there were massive waves at the beach that day. While I was swimming, there was this giant wave being formed and I was already in the deep and too far away from the shore to return. So I was staring at this wave coming straight at me, and the size of it started freaking me out. I did the only thing I knew to do: I swam towards it as fast as I could, and dove in and through it to the other side. I was fine.

Now, if you're a surfer, obviously your goal is to catch the wave and ride on top of it; but since I don't know how to surf, and for the sake of analogies here, I'll stick to what I know. What I want to talk about is for those of us that are in the water—and in particular, the water of life. We can encounter some pretty scary waves, scary seasons, and decisions that are daunting that we need to make or that we've already made. Often, our first instinct is to retreat and run away. However, I don't believe that's the kind of people that God made us to be.

The only way to go deeper into the ocean is to get past the waves that come crashing at you. In life, they can be waves of doubt, waves of memories taunting you of your past failure, or waves of the task before you that is way bigger than you and more than you even know how to handle. I remember just after I started Wings, it was as if every contradictory thought of inadequacy flooded my mind and hit me from every corner. I heard this voice in me asking, "What have you done?! What were you thinking?" I started second-guessing myself, being a single young lady stepping out like this. Even in your obedience to God, not everyone is going to be on your side or understand right away either. Pastor Erwin McManus said once, "You're not limited by what others don't know about you—about what God is doing inside you." At that point, the voices in my life that mattered most had been cheering me on to follow the steps God was leading me in. The bottom line was that I had heard from God and I knew what He wanted me to do. I was stepping out to follow what He was leading me into.

And for all of us, the truth is, the only way to go deeper and further into the ocean of purpose God has for us is to go through the wave right in front of us; embarking out into the unknown. In life, waves are always coming at us; sometimes in the form of blessings, and other times in the form of challenges. What I want to emphasize here is to not back down, run away, or curl up in a ball in fear when a giant wave of life comes at you. Don't back down, you have what it takes to get through it!

Whatever wave in life is coming at you today, I want to encourage you that the answer is not running away from things, and it's not staying in place either. God wants to give you the courage you need right now and build endurance in you as you decide to not back down. Keep pushing forward, and with courage, go through the wave in front of you!

Faith Food Authors:

Becca Giles - USA
Becky Blanchard - USA
Ben Lawalata - Indonesia
Chantel Garza - South Africa
David Blanchard - USA
Donna Blanchard - USA
Fero Permatasari - Indonesia
Ismael Garza - Mexico
Kelly Lawalata - USA
Kim Lunn - USA
Ria Lowing - Indonesia
Ricardo Rayon - Mexico
Rob Giles - USA
Rodney Richard - USA
Stephen Walter - USA
Steve Lunn - Hong Kong
Taryon Crawford - USA
Vanessa Birkbeck - Zimbabwe

About Wings International
"Giving Children Shoes to Run and Wings to Fly"

Shoes - Helping to provide for at-risk and underprivileged children of Asia with common necessities (food, housing, clothing, education, etc.) giving them the right footing in life.

Wings - Jesus wants to give all children wings to fly, so our aim is to provide them with the spiritual support needed to discover their God-given potential and purpose in life- so they can truly soar! This includes Children's discipleship teaching, counseling, healing and the like.

For more information visit:
www.wings-international.org